Standard Methods in the Art of Change Ringing

W. Pennington Bickford

Clement Danes

Strand . WC

1920

STANDARD METHODS

IN THE ART OF CHANGE RINGING.

BY THE LATE
JASPER W. SNOWDON.

Revised and Enlarged
BY
WM. SNOWDON,
President of the Yorkshire Association of Change Ringers.

LETTER-PRESS.

ALL MINOR, TRIPLE, AND MAJOR METHODS WITH IRREGULAR LEAD-ENDS OMITTED ;

ORDINARY METHODS PRODUCING '65S AT BACK-STROKE EXPUNGED ;

AND CORRECT EXAMPLES SUBSTITUTED ;

TOGETHER WITH A SELECTION OF
SEVEN GENUINE SURPRISE MINOR METHODS.

Complete with a Calling, in the letterpress portion, for the benefit of the young Conductor, of each Coloured Example, whether in Doubles, Minor, Triples, or Major.

ALL RIGHTS RESERVED.

PRICES :

The Complete Work	-	2s. 6d.
Diagrams Alone -	-	1s. 6d.
Letterpress Alone -	-	1s. 6d.

LEEDS :
FRED. R. SPARK & SON, CITY PRINTING WORKS, COOKRIDGE STREET.

1908.
To be obtained from the Editor, WM. SNOWDON, Civil Engineer, Leeds.

CONTENTS OF LETTERPRESS.

PREFACE, BIBLIOGRAPHY, AND GLOSSARY

Advertisements will be found with the Diagrams

PREFACE TO THE REVISED EDITION.

So great a favourite has my brother's book, "Standard Methods," been in the past that no apology need be made for this fifth edition.

As, however, it has proved necessary to greatly revise the work, some explanation is due to those who may feel disappointed in not securing the same set of methods which have been heretofore in circulation.

It has long been known—even to my brother in his life-time—that many superior methods might have been chosen, but alterations have been postponed time after time for the sake of uniformity ; in fact, the book has been viewed, latterly, more as a text book for the learner than as an authority on the point of what should constitute a sound method.

This state of affairs could not continue, of course, and now a systematic attempt has been made to bring all into line with the advanced thought of the day ; the new purchaser, therefore, will find—it is trusted—that he is now buying the book of the future, and not of the past.

Three special efforts have been made : first, to insert only such even-bell methods as produce the lead-ends of Plain-Bob in the plain course—when of that character ; secondly, to reject, as far as possible, all Minor Methods turning up '65 at back-stroke ; and lastly, to supply Seven Surprise Minor Methods of as true a Surprise character as repeated researches point to as possible.

Dealing with the first point :—Endeavours were made 200 years ago, for correct lead-ends, a notable one being the alteration of "College Bob V.," of 1677, to "Westminster," in 1702; the only alteration necessary to bring the figures into correct form being the substitution of third's place for fifth's, with the treble behind. But, alas, no sustained endeavour followed, and even such a careful observer as my brother seems to have contented himself by the addition of marks of admiration, in his note-books, to those methods which had the desired lead-ends—probably the matter was not ripe in his day for the advance now demanded by the leading members of our Central Council. One more example of careless lead-ends may be interesting :—When Cambridge Surprise Major first appeared in print in 1766, its lead-ends were irregular, and it was left for the " *Clavis*," in 1788, to put the matter right, and to hand it down to us in good order.

The second point :—The avoidance of Minor Methods with '65 at back-stroke : This is intimately—although not entirely—connected with correct lead-ends. There is a tendency to think that ordinary methods with correct lead-ends are so far safe that the '65s at back-stroke may be left to take care of themselves, but it is not so, for London Treble Bob Minor had correct lead-ends, and yet it turned up six '65s at back-stroke in the 720. But the worst and greatest offender is our old favourite " Duke of York," for not only did it transgress with its irregular lead-ends, but, out of the twenty-four possible, it produced eighteen of these discordant '65s at back-stroke ; in fact, the only correct '56s are those at the three part-ends, where the conductor positively " *calls* " these bells to behave properly at the full lead and dodge, which close the division ! It is foreign to our immediate purpose to allude here to the mistaken custom that many six-bell companies have in the North, of ringing without the open lead at hand, but we cannot pass without claiming for the county, which loves the " Duke of York," that it is distinctly a musical part of our country, hence possibly its six-bell ringers have dropped the open-leads to improve the music of bad methods ! If so, the endeavour to banish '65s at back should do good in this direction. The mathematical music of our bells demands punctuation to bring out its rhythm, and all to the contrary is monotonous, and unworthy of the Art in the opinion of every writer that has touched upon the subject.

The third aim of the work, viz., the selection of seven genuine Surprise Minor Methods, has been a difficult one, for it necessitated much analytical investigation to gain a true understanding of the points that constitute a Surprise Method. Even some experts who correctly hold that treble bob behaviour at the cross-sections, viz., where the treble passes from one dodging place to another, at once destroys all claim to the title of Surprise—(as witness the general agreement as to Coventry, erroneously, with many others, dubbed Surprise in the " *Clavis* ")—seem to think lightly of treble bob work introduced at the *two greatest cross-sections of all,* viz., when the treble leads and lies ! No such loose notions have been allowed to creep in here, and every extreme position of the treble, fore and aft, has been treated after the manner of Cambridge and London Surprise, that is to say, with correct *internal* places. An important advance in method building and composition might be termed a " Triumph," when it cannot be classed as a Surprise.

Cambridge, London, York, and Beverley, all behave perfectly in the matter of their '65s at back, but, alas, Carlisle, Chester, and Canterbury assert their Surprise disabilities, and turn up '65 twice in a part, or six times in a 720. Having spent a considerable amount of time in experimenting as to the possibility or otherwise of avoiding these blemishes, the Author's old friends, Messrs. Penning and Pitstow were written to, asking whether they could throw any further light on the subject. Curiously, my brother had, it appears, corresponded with them on this same point when busy with the matter that now forms page 71—fifth edition—of " Ropesight." Their very instructive reply—if put into short language—stands substantially thus: Even if with correct lead-ends, you have a method that still insists upon sending the tenors behind, in the plain course, in an order unknown in the plain course of Bob Minor, look out for squalls! With this terse way of summing up—and with many thanks for it—the question may be left for the reader's further examination. A word of caution may assist those seeking for true daylight in Surprise matters: Canterbury Surprise differs from what was previously known as Canterbury Bob; the difference may be slight, but there it is, and it prevents " stagnation " behind.

I have to thank Sir Arthur Heywood for his permission to make extracts from his book on " Duffield." This method is a very musical one, and should be kept alive, especially by ten and twelve bell towers where the tenor is not too heavy to turn in. To Mr. John Carter my thanks are also due for letters and explanations, for I could not make headway with his new principle at first sight. That all is now quite plain is my hope.

It is, we fear, quite impossible to have escaped all errors in such a difficult revision as this, and we need hardly say how grateful we shall be to anyone pointing out any improvements for the next edition, and, alas, any inconsistences, if such there be, that may have slipped in.

Leeds, December, 1908.   WM. SNOWDON.

LIST OF BOOKS QUOTED FROM OR EXAMINED.

(Stedman's Tintinnalogia	A.D.	1668)
Stedman's Campanalogia		1677
Campanalogia, by J.D. & C.M.		1702
(Ditto. Second Edition		1705)
Ditto Third ,, ...		1733
Ditto Fourth ,, First gives Cambridge Surprise Minor		1753
Ditto Fifth (Monk's) Edition, First gives Cambridge Surprise Major		1766
Clavis Campanalogia, by Jones, Reeves and Blakemore		1788
Ditto Ditto Second Edition		1796
Shipway's Work		1816
Hubbard's Work		1845
(And subsequently in 1854, 1864, 1868, and 1875).		
Thackrah's Work		1852
Sottanstall's Work		1867
Bannister's Work		1874
Heywood's " Duffield "		1888

Of the above the first and fourth, shown in brackets, are not on the Editor's shelves, but they have been included in the list for bibliographical purposes.

GLOSSARY.

This is only a shortened list; nearly everything will explain itself by referring the text to the diagram; terms vary somewhat with different methods.

CHAP. I.—THE PLAIN BOB METHOD.

(Dates from Stedman's time)

THE underlying principle of this is plain hunting, except when the treble leads; the bell then turned from the lead makes second's place, and the others dodge. Plain Bob, though primarily an "*even bell*" method, is adaptable to odd numbers; in these cases, when the treble leads, the bell behind, having no one to dodge with, lies four blows there.

Plain Bob is best rung by noticing where each bell passes the treble, and learning the relative order in which the variations from plain hunting follow one another, as below.

Beginners requiring further explanations are referred to Snowdon's "*Ropesight.*"

All numbers on the left of the rules refer to the different leads—first lead, second lead, and so on; and the duty appearing in the same line relatively corresponds.

BOB DOUBLES; *Diagram page* 1.

Duty of each bell, after making second's place.

1.—Turn the treble from behind .. Dodge in 3-4 down.
2.—Pass the treble in 3-4 .... Lie four blows behind.
3.—Pass the treble in 2-3 .... Dodge in 3-4 up.
4.—Treble turns you from the lead, Make second's place, and lead again.

The following example shows how a bob is made; fourth's place being made instead of second's place:

$$
\begin{array}{c}
3\ 5\ 2\ 4\ 1 \\
3\ 2\ 5\ 1\ 4 \\
2\ 3\ 1\ 5\ 4 \\
2\ 1\ 3\ 4\ 5 \\
\text{Bob} \left\{ \begin{array}{c} 1\ 2\ 4\ 3\ 5 \\ 1\ 4\ 2\ 3\ 5 \end{array} \right. \\
\hline
4\ 1\ 3\ 2\ 5 \\
4\ 3\ 1\ 5\ 2
\end{array}
$$

As a bob causes an alteration in the work of the bells in front only, the following table of these alterations will serve for this and any other number of bells :

A bob alters the work of the bells thus :

A bell, that would have made second's place, runs out quick.

A bell, that would have dodged in 3-4 down, runs in quick.

A bell, that would have dodged in 3-4 up, makes fourth's place and goes down to lead again, and is said to "make the bob."

Bob Minor ; *Diagram page 2.*

Duty of each bell, after making second's place.

1.—Turn the treble from behind   .Dodge in 3-4 down.
2 —Pass the treble in 4-5   ......Dodge in 5-6 down. after lying full.
3.—Pass the treble in 3-4   .. ...Dodge in 5-6 up, before lying full.
4 —Pass the treble in 2-3   .. ...Dodge in 3-4 up.
5 —Treble turns you from the lead, Make second's place, and lead again.

On six bells another alteration, in addition to the Bob, is required. This is called a " Single," and is made by the bells in second's, third's, and fourth's places, lying still. As the bells above fourth's place are not altered by a Single, the three following rules embrace the different duties, of the bells concerned in such a call, on any number of bells :

The duty of the Bells at a Single.

A bell. turned from the lead by the treble. makes second's place, and leads again, as at a plain lead.

A bell. that would have dodged in 3-4 up, makes fourth's place, and goes down to lead again, thus doing " the bob work of the single."

A bell, that turned the treble from behind, and would have dodged in 3-4 down. makes third's place, and then hunts up again, and is said to " make the single."

Examples of a bob, and single, follow the plain course diagram.

Bob Triples* ; *Diagram page 22.*

Duty of each bell, after making second's place.

1 —Turn the treble from behind .. Dodge in 3-4 down.
2.—Pass the treble in 5-6 .. . ... Dodge in 5-6 down.
3.—Pass the treble in 4-5   .. .   Lie four blows behind.
4.—Pass the treble in 3-4 .... Dodge in 5-6 up.
5 —Pass the treble in 2-3 .... Dodge in 3-4 up.
6.—Treble turns you from the lead, Make second's place, and lead again.

Examples of a bob, and single, are here given :

$$2\ 1\ 3\ 4\ 5\ 6\ 7 \qquad\qquad 2\ 1\ 3\ 4\ 5\ 6\ 7$$

Bob $\begin{cases} 1\ 2\ 4\ 3\ 6\ 5\ 7 \\ 1\ 4\ 2\ 3\ 5\ 6\ 7 \end{cases}$ Single $\begin{cases} 1\ 2\ 4\ 3\ 6\ 5\ 7 \\ 1\ 2\ 4\ 3\ 5\ 6\ 7 \end{cases}$

$$4\ 1\ 3\ 2\ 6\ 5\ 7 \qquad\qquad 2\ 1\ 3\ 4\ 6\ 5\ 7$$

Bob Major ; *Diagram page 24*

Duty of each bell, after making second's place.

1.—Turn the treble from behind   . Dodge in 3-4 down.
2 —Pass the treble in 6-7 .... . Dodge in 5-6 down.
3 —Pass the treble in 5-6 .... Dodge in 7-8 down.
4.—Pass the treble in 4-5 ...   Dodge in 7-8 up.
5.—Pass the treble in 3-4 .   ... Dodge in 5-6 up.
6.—Pass the treble in 2-3   . . .. Dodge in 3-4 up.
7.—Treble turns you from the lead, Make second's place, and lead again.

Examples of a bob, and single, follow the plain course diagram.

---

* These are now considered irregular, but they are quite justifiable as a step, for the beginner, between Minor and Major. Grandsire Doubles and Triples are undoubtedly much more musical than the Doubles and Triples of Plain Bob, and that alone should settle the question.—Ed.

CHAP. II.—THE GRANDSIRE METHOD.

(Dates from Stedman's time.)

In this the treble has a plain hunting path, and so likewise have all the bells, except when the treble is at the lead. The bell turned from the lead by the treble makes third's place, and the others, behind, dodge.

The peculiarity of the method is that one bell, namely, that which courses after the treble, is not interrupted in its work either by the place-making or dodging, but continues to hunt up and down after the treble. This bell (the second in the plain course) is said to be " *in the hunt with the treble*," or, more briefly, " *in the hunt*." The bell making the third's place at each lead-end is said to be " *before ;* " and the bells behind are said to dodge in 4-5 up, 4-5 down, and so on.

Like Plain Bob, it is rung by the course method, and by observing in which place each bell, after leaving the lead, passes the treble.

Grandsire commences on five bells, and although primarily an odd-bell method, may be rung on even numbers. In giving the rules for ringing the method, as, in the plain course, the second is in the hunt, the duty will be commenced from the position of a bell after making third's place. In

Grandsire, on account of the bell in the hunt, a plain course consists of one treble lead less than usual in other methods.

GRANDSIRE DOUBLES ; *Diagram page* 1.

Duty of each bell, after making third's place.

1.—Pass the treble in 3-4 .... Dodge in 4-5 down, after lying full.

2.—Pass the treble in 2-3 .... Dodge in 4-5 up, before lying full.

3.—Treble turns you from the lead, Make third's place, and lead again.

With regard to the practical ringing of Grandsire, a beginner should remember, in coming down after each lead-end, the following important directions :—

When making third's place, the last blow in third's will be over the treble.

After dodging in 4-5 down, the first bell to take, on the way down, is the treble.

After dodging in 4-5 up, the last blow of the whole pull behind will be over the treble.

After taking the treble, either in going up or down, the next blow will be over the bell in the hunt.

If, when out of the tower, a beginner will carefully study these directions, and afterwards pay attention to them when ringing, it is obvious that, in the plain course of Grandsire Doubles, as he will know when to strike over the treble, and the bell in the hunt (the second), there remain the movements of two bells only which he need specially watch.

To facilitate reference to the figures in the foregoing and following remarks, plain, bob, and single leads are given over-leaf.

A bob in Grandsire requires a third's place to be made before the treble has fully led, in addition to the ordinary third's place when the treble has done leading. Two third's places are thus made at a bob, and the bells making these third's places are, respectively, said to make the "*first third's*" and "*last third's*."* The first third's compels the bells then behind to dodge ; and, that, in the places previous to those in which they would have so done had no call been made ; and the last third's causes them to repeat this dodge. At a bob, therefore, the bells behind make a double dodge, and commence such dodging a whole pull earlier than they would otherwise have done. (*See foot note, page* 14.)

PLAIN LEAD :	BOB LEAD :	SINGLE LEAD :
4 3 5 2 1	4 3 5 2 1	4 3 5 2 1
4 5 3 1 2	4 5 3 1 2	4 5 3 1 2
5 4 1 3 2	5 4 1 3 2	5 4 1 3 2
5 1 4 2 3	5 1 4 2 3	5 1 4 2 3
1 5 2 4 3	1 5 4 3 2	1 5 4 3 2
1 2 5 3 4	1 4 5 2 3	1 5 4 2 3
2 1 5 4 3	4 1 5 3 2	5 1 4 3 2
2 5 1 3 4	4 5 1 2 3	5 4 1 2 3
5 2 3 1 4	5 4 2 1 3	4 5 2 1 3
5 3 2 4 1	5 2 4 3 1	4 2 5 3 1

An ordinary Grandsire single is made by the bells in second's and third's places lying still ; that is, the bell that the treble turns from the lead makes second's place, and the bell that makes first third's also makes last third's—thus striking four blows in third's place. The bells behind make a double dodge, as at a bob, and commence dodging a whole pull earlier than at a plain lead.

Both at a bob and a single, *the bell in the hunt* has its plain hunting course stopped, and is compelled, further, to make a double dodge in 4-5 down, and take its place amongst the other " inside " bells ; it is then said to " *come out of the hunt.*" The ringer who makes the first third's at a bob, or the second's place at a single, must remember that his bell then " *goes into the hunt.*" A bob therefore alters the duty of every bell, with the exception of the one that makes last third's. The following rules for making a bob in Grandsire Doubles should therefore be committed to memory.

A bob alters the work of the bells thus :—

(*a*) A bell, in the hunt makes a double dodge in 4-5 down, and comes out of the hunt.

(*b*) A bell, that would have dodged in 4-5 down, makes a double dodge in 4-5 up, with the bell that comes out of the hunt.

(*c*) A bell, that would have dodged in 4-5 up, makes first third's, that is, " makes the bob," goes down to lead, and becomes the bell in the hunt.

At a single the work of every bell is altered, two doing duty as at a bob.

A single alters the work of the bells thus :—

(*a*) A bell in the hunt " comes out," as at a bob.

(*b*) A bell due to dodge in 4-5 down behaves as at a bob.

(*c*) A bell, that would have dodged in 4-5 up, strikes four blows in third's place, does " the bob work of a single," and goes down to lead.

(*d*) A bell turned from the lead by the treble, and that would have made third's place, makes second's place, leads again, and becomes the bell in the hunt, and is said to " make the single."

Besides learning these rules, each beginner should observe, from the figures, where he will first strike over the treble after completing the work at a bob, or a single. He will thus see that the bells in 4-5 continue dodging until separated by the treble, and he will also learn how to make other useful notes for his guidance when ringing. Each one should also make himself acquainted with the work he will do at the lead following a bob, or a single lead, whether such be a plain, bob, or single lead.

GRANDSIRE MINOR* ; *Diagram page 5.*

Duty of each bell, after making third's place.

1.—Pass the treble in 4-5 .... Dodge in 4-5 down.
2.—Pass the treble in 3-4 .... Lie four blows behind.
3.—Pass the treble in 2-3 .... Dodge in 4-5 up.
4.—Treble turns you from the lead, Make third's place, and lead again.

In ringing Grandsire on even numbers, a bell lies four blows behind at each plain lead. At a bob, or single, the bell that would have dodged in 4-5 down, lies six blows behind, as in the following examples taken from the first lead :—

PLAIN LEAD :	BOB LEAD :	SINGLE LEAD :
4 6 3 5 2 1	4 6 3 5 2 1	4 6 3 5 2 1
6 4 5 3 1 2	6 4 5 3 1 2	6 4 5 3 1 2
6 5 4 1 3 2	6 5 4 1 3 2	6 5 4 1 3 2
5 6 1 4 2 3	5 6 1 4 2 3	5 6 1 4 2 3
5 1 6 2 4 3	5 1 6 2 4 3	5 1 6 2 4 3
1 5 2 6 3 4	1 5 6 4 2 3	1 5 6 4 2 3
1 2 5 3 6 4	1 6 5 2 4 3	1 5 6 2 4 3
2 1 5 6 3 4	6 1 5 4 2 3	5 1 6 4 2 3
2 5 1 3 6 4	6 5 1 2 4 3	5 6 1 2 4 3
5 2 3 1 4 6	5 6 2 1 3 4	6 5 2 1 3 4
5 3 2 4 1 6	5 2 6 3 1 4	6 2 5 3 1 4
3 5 4 2 6 1	2 5 3 6 4 1	2 6 3 5 4 1

As it is improbable that any company of ringers will practise Grandsire Minor without having first made themselves acquainted with Doubles ; and as the rules for bobs

---

* Now considered irregular, but an allowable educational step between Grandsire Doubles and Triples notwithstanding.—ED

and singles in Minor are almost the same, I do not think it necessary to go over the ground again.

GRANDSIRE TRIPLES ; *Diagram page 22.*

Duty of each bell, after making third's place.

1.—Pass the treble in 5-6 ....Dodge in 4-5 down.
2.—Pass the treble in 4-5 ....Dodge in 6-7 down.
3 —Pass the treble in 3-4 ....Dodge in 6-7 up.
4.—Pass the treble in 2-3 ....Dodge in 4-5 up.
5.—Treble turns you from the lead, Make third's place, and lead again.

The duty of each bell in Grandsire Triples is merely an extension of that already explained for Doubles. The bobs and singles are also made according to the same rules.

PLAIN LEAD :	BOB LEAD :	SINGLE LEAD :
6 4 7 3 5 2 1	6 4 7 3 5 2 1	6 4 7 3 5 2 1
6 7 4 5 3 1 2	6 7 4 5 3 1 2	6 7 4 5 3 1 2
7 6 5 4 1 3 2	7 6 5 4 1 3 2	7 6 5 4 1 3 2
7 5 6 1 4 2 3	7:5 6 1 4 2 3	7 5 6 1 4 2 3
5 7 1 6 2 4 3	5 7 1 6 2 4 3	5 7 1 6 2 4 3
5 1 7 2 6 3 4	5 1 7 2 6 3 4	5 1 7 2 6 3 4
1 5 2 7 3 6 4	1 5 7 6 2 4 3	1 5 7 6 2 4 3
1 2 5 3 7 4 6	1 7 5 2 6 3 4	1 5 7 2 6 3 4
2 1 5 7 3 6 4	7 1 5 6 2 4 3	5 1 7 6 2 4 3
2 5 1 3 7 4 6	7 5 1 2 6 3 4	5 7 1 2 6 3 4
5 2 3 1 4 7 6	5 7 2 1 3 6 4	7 5 2 1 3 6 4
5 3 2 4 1 6 7	5 2 7 3 1 4 6	7 2 5 3 1 4 6
3 5 4 2 6 1 7	2 5 3 7 4 1 6	2 7 3 5 4 1 6
3 4 5 6 2 7 1	2 3 5 4 7 6 1	2 3 7 4 5 6 1

A bob alters the work of bells thus :

A bell, in the hunt, makes a double dodge in 4-5 down, and leaves the hunt.
A bell, due to dodge in 4-5 down, makes a double dodge in 6-7 down.
A bell, due to dodge in 6-7 down, makes a double dodge in 6-7 up.
A bell, due to dodge in 6-7 up, makes a double dodge in 4-5 up.
A bell, due to dodge in 4-5 up, makes first third's, and enters the hunt.

At an ordinary single, a bell, turned from the lead by the treble, makes second's place, and, leading again, becomes the bell in the hunt; a bell making first third's, also makes second third's, and leads again; whilst the pairs behind make a double dodge.

Besides this ordinary single there is another which is sometimes used in Grandsire Triples. In this, which is known as a "*Holt's Single,*" the bells in fourth's, fifth's, sixth's, and seventh's places lie still. The singles are used in Holt's six-part and ten-part peals, and as these are often rung it may prove useful to have examples. I therefore give them as they usually occur, namely, one at the end of the first half-peal, and the other at the coming round.

Single (Bob) used in Holt's Ten-Part Peal.

First Half-Peal End.	Last Half-peal End.
5 7 2 6 3 4 1	4 6 2 7 3 5 1
5 2 7 3 6 1 4	4 2 6 3 7 1 5
2 5 3 7 1 6 4	2 4 3 6 1 7 5
2 3 5 1 7 4 6	2 3 4 1 6 5 7
3 2 1 5 4 7 6	3 2 1 4 5 6 7
3 1 2 4 5 6 7	3 1 2 5 4 7 6
1 3 2 5 4 7 6	1 3 2 4 5 6 7
1 2 3 5 4 7 6	1 2 3 4 5 6 7
2 1 3 4 5 6 7	2 1 3 5 4 7 6
2 3 1 5 4 7 6	2 3 1 4 5 6 7
3 2 5 1 7 4 6	3 2 4 1 6 5 7
3 5 2 7 1 6 4	3 4 2 6 1 7 5
5 3 7 2 6 1 4	4 3 6 2 7 1 5
5 7 3 6 2 4 1	4 6 3 7 2 5 1

SINGLES (PLAIN-LEAD) USED IN HOLT'S SIX-PART PEAL.

FIRST HALF-PEAL END.	LAST HALF-PEAL END.
7 6 5 4 3 2 1	6 7 4 5 3 2 1
7 5 6 3 4 1 2	6 4 7 3 5 1 2
5 7 3 6 1 4 2	4 6 3 7 1 5 2
5 3 7 1 6 2 4	4 3 6 1 7 2 5
3 5 1 7 2 6 4	3 4 1 6 2 7 5
3 1 5 2 7 4 6	3 1 4 2 6 5 7
1 3 2 5 4 7 6	1 3 2 4 5 6 7
1 2 3 5 4 7 6	1 2 3 4 5 6 7
2 1 3 4 5 6 7	2 1 3 5 4 7 6
2 3 1 5 4 7 6	2 3 1 4 5 6 7
3 2 5 1 7 4 6	3 2 4 1 6 5 7
3 5 2 7 1 6 4	3 4 2 6 1 7 5
5 3 7 2 6 1 4	4 3 6 2 7 1 5
5 7 3 6 2 4 1	4 6 3 7 2 5 1

At the last half-peal-end, the single brings the bells round; the changes which are, for symmetry, given after this point are, in reality, those with which the peal commences.*

CHAP. III.—THE TREBLE BOB SYSTEM.

OXFORD, *dates from* 1677; AND KENT, *from* 1788.

TREBLE BOB is not well adapted for practice on a less number than six. The simplest, or primary methods, on which the system is founded, are known as Oxford, and Kent; and as they are so frequently practised I shall here explain them

---

* Snowdon's "Grandsire" should be consulted by those desiring further information.—ED.

both. Before, however, proceeding to lay down rules for ringing them, I must call attention to the zig-zag hunting course of the treble, peculiar to all Treble Bob methods.

This, although perfectly uniform in each treble lead, is totally different from the straight hunting course in Plain Bob, and Grandsire, and it is therefore the first thing with which a ringer has to make himself acquainted.

Reference to any of the Treble Bob Minor diagrams (pages 6 to 21), will show that the treble dodges in each place in its progress up and down. Thus, after leading the whole pull (or, in fewer words, leading full), the treble strikes one blow in second's place, and, dodging back, strikes another blow at the lead. It then hunts up into fourth's, and dodges back into third's; hunts up behind, and, striking one blow there, dodges back into fifth's, and then lies full. After this it strikes one blow in fifth's, and dodges back into sixth's; then hunts down into third's, and dodges back into fourth's; then hunts down to the lead, and, striking one blow there, dodges back into second's place, and then leads full.

The technical way of expressing this is as follows : The treble is said to *dodge on the lead* after leading full ; to *dodge in the middle going up ;* to *dodge behind* before lying full ; and, similarly, on the way down, to dodge behind after lying full ; to dodge in the middle going down ; and to dodge on the lead before leading full.

On any number of bells, above six, the intermediate dodgings are known by the different places in which they occur ; thus on eight bells, the terms " *dodging in 3-4,*" and " *dodging in 5-6,*" up, or down, as the case may be, are used.

Every beginner, before he attempts Treble Bob, should learn to count the places into which he will fall, on the way from the lead to the back, and down again, and thus thoroughly acquaint himself with what is called a " *Treble Bob hunt.*"

Since the treble strikes two blows in each place, it follows that a treble lead contains twice the number of changes to be found in a plain hunt lead on the same number of bells.

In each treble lead of Oxford, and Kent, as well as in many other variations, there is one bell which has a special path. If the first lead of the diagram of Oxford, or Kent, be referred to, it will be seen that the second bell, after dodging with the treble, leads full, and makes second's place, alternately, until the treble returns to the lead. This bell is called the " *slow hunt,*" and is said to be " *in the hunt,*" or, more appropriately, as there is no hunting, " *in the slow.*"

In the methods under notice, the working of the slow bell prevents others dodging on the lead, nevertheless, with this exception, and those caused by the place-making (which will be explained hereafter), the " inside bells " work in a similar way to the treble, and are then said to be doing oridnary " *Treble Bob work.*"

The place-making, and the complications arising thereout, give the different degrees of intricacy to the various Treble Bob methods.

OXFORD TREBLE BOB MINOR ; *Diagram page* 6.

The simplicity of this method is due to the fact that places are made only when the treble is dodging on the lead before and after leading full. At these times the bells in the middle, instead of dodging, make, respectively, third's,

and fourth's places. The annexed changes represent the
place-making at the end of the first treble lead
of Oxford T. B. Minor. The places made when
the treble dodges, before leading full, are called
" *first third's,*" and " *first fourth's,*" and those
made when the treble dodges, after leading full,
are called " *last third's,*" and " *last fourth's.*"*
This place-making reverses the direction in which
the bells are coursing ; that is, the bell that, in
hunting up, makes fourth's place, *then* goes down
again to the lead ; and, *vice versa*, the bell that, in
going down, makes third's place, goes up again behind.

```
4 2 5 1 6 3
2 4 1 5 3 6
2 1 4 3 5 6
1 2 3 4 6 5
2 1 3 4 5 6
1 2 4 3 6 5
1 4 2 6 3 5
4 1 6 2 5 3
1 4 6 2 3 5
4 1 2 6 5 3
4 2 1 5 6 3
2 4 5 1 3 6
```

By referring to the diagram the path of the second bell
in a plain course may be examined and its duty carefully
studied. The ringer of this bell, on going off, strikes one
blow at the lead, and dodges back into second's place ; in
other words, he dodges with the treble. He then, alternately,
leads full, and makes second's place, until the treble returns
to him ; he then dodges with her, and so completes the slow
work. On leaving the slow work he makes fourth's place
(last fourth's) and returns to the lead. He leads full, and
then hunts up in the ordinary Treble Bob manner. After
this he hunts down into third's, but here the ordinary Treble
Bob work is broken by his being compelled—the treble being
at the lead—to make third's place (first third's), and to hunt
up behind. During the next two leads he does the ordinary
work of an inside bell in Treble Bob. This continues until
he enters upon the fifth lead, and finds the treble in front

* " First," and " last," as here used, refer to the work then being done by the
treble in front, and not to the whole lead.

when he reaches third's place (for this position of the treble he will have been prepared by noticing that he had previously passed her in 4-5), hence he is compelled to make this third's place (second third's) and return behind. He then does ordinary work until he leads full. Now he will pass the treble in 2-3, make fourth's place (first fourth's), and go down to lead, where he will dodge with the treble, and again take up the slow work.

With regard to the course method for Oxford, it will be seen, by the diagram, that, after a bell has been in the slow, the other leads of the plain course may be divided, thus :—

In the opening of the lead, after doing the slow work, you make last fourth's and down, and, at the close, make first third's and up ; this may be termed a " *place-making lead.*" During the next two leads the ordinary Treble Bob work is unbroken, but the following (the fifth) is another place-making lead ; that is, at the opening, last third's, and, at the close, first fourth's are made ; after which you again take up the slow work,

In the two *intermediate leads* (between the place-making leads) each ringer should notice that, in the first of them, he dodges with the treble in the middle, going up, and (in consequence of his work behind being the same as that of the treble in front) in the second of them, he again dodges with her in the middle on his way down. By observing how the work thus progresses a ringer gains confidence, and, after dodging with the treble—as last mentioned—on his way down, will be prepared to again meet her on his way up in 4-5 ; and on going down again he will, as the diagram has proved, enter a place-making lead, and make third's place, etc. The foregoing directions may be condensed thus :—

Rules for the course method in Oxford T. B. Minor.

1.—Slow work.
2.—Last fourth's and down ; and later, first third's and up.
3.—Dodge, with the treble, in the middle, going up.
4.—Dodge, with the treble, in the middle, coming down ; and, on the way up, pass the treble in 4-5.
5.—Last third's and up ; and later, first fourth's, and into the slow.

Although at first it may appear that the dodges in Treble Bob require special quickness of sight, this is not actually the case, because the selection of the bell to follow, is more easily made than in plain methods, as will now be shown.

It will be seen that, when dodging, a bell strikes twice over another. Take for example, the treble in 3-4 going up in the first lead (diagram p. 6) The first blow in fourth's is *over the sixth*, the dodging blow into third's is over the last of the two bells below (the bell in the slow), and the next blow in fourth's is again *over the sixth*. When the treble is going behind, the work is still easier, because two blows are struck twice over the same two bells ; for example, the treble strikes her blows in fifth's, and sixth's, over the fifth, and fourth, and then dodges back over the fifth, and again follows the fourth. This applies to all the different dodging places and to all the bells, with the exception of certain alterations when the places are being made ; the bells behind at these points will then find that they strike over different bells when they strike their two blows in fifth's.

When making fourth's place each bell strikes two consecutive blows over the one making third's. When making third's place each learner should know *which* of the blows *must* be over the treble. My meaning is this :—When the third's places are made, the treble and another are in front ; and when the first third's is made the treble is leading at hand, and dodging into second's place at back-stroke. The ringer who makes the first third's, should, therefore, guided by this knowledge, first strike *after the other bell*, and then *after the treble*. In like manner, when making last third's, he will, first, strike *after the treble*, and then *after the other bell*.

A learner should, by a careful study of the path of a bell, be able to count each place into which he will fall throughout a course, before he attempts to ring it. Oxford is, however, so simple that if anyone forgets his exact place, in the course, he may always put himself right by remembering, on going into 3-4, that if the treble be in front he must make a place instead of dodging, and then retrace his steps.

A bob (diagram p. 6) is made thus :—The bell that makes the first third's then makes fourth's place and also the last third's, and hunts up. The bells behind make a double dodge in addition to the ordinary one.

A bob does not alter the bells entering or leaving the slow work. The bell that " *makes the bob* " (the one that makes third's, fourth's and third's) has its work thrown on two leads ; that is, it omits the two " intermediate leads," and therefore, at the end of the lead thus opened, it makes first fourth's and takes up the slow work. The bells behind, which makes the double dodge in addition to the ordinary one, have their work retarded a lead ; that is, during the next lead they repeat the work of the previous one.

The proper time to call " bob " is when the treble strikes its *first* blow at the lead. The bell that has lain full behind can then count three dodging blows back into sixth's, and the bell that has yet to lie full can count three into fifth's. Those behind should notice that the three blows struck into fifth's are, in turn, over the other "inside" bells.

KENT TREBLE BOB MINOR; *Diagram page* 7.

The foregoing explanation of Oxford applies almost exactly to Kent. The only difference between the two is in the place-making. As before, places are made when the treble is dodging in front, but instead of *one* place being made by each of the bells in 3-4, *two* are made, and the bells continue coursing in their previous paths. Thus, as will be seen in the annexed figures, when the treble dodges at the lead *before* leading full, "*first third's and fourth's*" are made by the bell hunting up, and "*first fourth's and third's*" by the bell hunting down. When the treble dodges *after* leading full "*last third's and fourth's*" and "*last fourth's and third's*" are made.

325164
231546
213456
123465
214356
124365
142635
412653
146235
416253
461523
645132

There is another point in which the place-making differs from Oxford, which must be carefully borne in mind. In Oxford the places are made at hand-and-back strokes, whereas in Kent they occur at back-and-hand. As the place-making, however, occurs at the same points in the plain course, the rules for Oxford are very easily adapted to Kent.

Rules for the course method in Kent T. B. Minor.

1.—Slow work.

2.—Last third's and fourth's and up; and first third's and fourth's and up.

3.—Dodge, with the treble, in the middle, going up.

4.—Dodge, with the treble, in the middle coming down; and, on the way up, pass the treble in 4-5.

5.—Last fourth's and third's and down; and first fourth's and third's and down into the slow work.

A bob (diagram p. 7) is made thus :—The bell that makes the *first* third's and fourth's, then makes *last* fourth's and third's, and goes down to lead. This bell, therefore, strikes four consecutive blows in fourth's. The bells behind make a double dodge in addition to the ordinary one.

A bob does not affect the bells entering, or leaving, the slow work, and the alterations caused in the work of the others, in the next lead, are, respectively, similar to those in Oxford. Ringers behind at a bob should remember that two of the blows struck in fifth's are over the same bell.

TREBLE BOB MAJOR.

OXFORD ; *Diagram pages* 28-29. KENT ; *Diagram pages* 30-31.

The only difference between Minor and Major in these two variations is the additional dodging place. Instead of having to dodge only in the middle, each bell has now additional dodges, in 3-4, and 5-6, on the way up, and down. In Major the place-making, as in Minor, is confined to 3-4 ; and it also occurs in the leads before and after that of the slow work. Two additional " intermediate leads," in which the bells do ordinary Treble Bob work, make up the seven leads which are contained in a plain course. The duty in Major is, thus, to one who can ring Minor, very easily learnt, and the practical rope-sight soon acquired.

Bobs (see diagrams) are made in each method, respectively, in the same way as in Minor ; the bells in 5-6 and 7-8 each dodging twice in addition to the ordinary dodge.

Care must be taken, as in Minor, when in 5-6, either at a plain, or a Bob lead, to observe when place-making is going on in 3-4, so as to select the right bells to strike after for the blows in fifth's place.

CHAP. IV.—STEDMAN'S PRINCIPLE.

This is founded on the two different peals, or "*sixes*," that can be rung on three bells. These sixes, which are given below, with their hand-and-back strokes bracketed, should therefore be carefully studied. It will then be seen that, in the first, the bells lead full at hand-and-back, and, in the latter, at back-and-hand ; that is, the ringers "*come to lead at hand*" and "*come to lead at back-stroke*." This leading is also known as "*leading full, right*," and "*leading full, wrong*."

Quick Six.	Slow Six.
1 2 3	1 2 3
2 1 3	1 3 2
2 3 1	3 1 2
3 2 1	3 2 1
3 1 2	2 3 1
1 3 2	2 1 3
1 2 3	1 2 3

Stedman's principle consists in the three bells in front ringing first one and then the other of these peals, whilst those above thirds are employing themselves in, what may be termed, a double dodging hunt, extending from 4-5, up, to the back, and down again to 4-5. It should be rung on odd numbers, as the bells behind then dodge, in pairs, in 4-5, 6-7, and so on. Each time that the three bells in front complete a six, one of them leaves the front and, going up, enters the "double dodging hunt," whilst the bell that has just completed the hunt comes down and joins the bells in front. In this way the bells are passed down into, and passed up out of, the sixes, and different changes are produced.

The point, at which one six ends, and the next begins, forms the *parting of the sixes ;* and at these two changes the bell behind lies full, wrong (back-and-hand).

STEDMAN'S DOUBLES ; *Diagram page* 40.

(Dates from Stedman's time.)

In pricking or ringing this system one naturally inquires how one should begin, and which six should be taken first.

These questions Steadman settled, in a manner easily remembered, by making the " go off " similar to that of Grandsire. If the first three changes of Stedman's Doubles be compared with those of Grandsire (diagram, p. 1) they will be found to be the same. But on comparing the front bells with the " go off " of the sixes given on the previous page, headed " quick " and " slow," no complete similarity will be found with either ; hence it may be inferred that a commencement has not been made with the first change of either six. If now it is noted that Stedman allowed the treble to run straight out into fourth's at the third change, it is plainly seen that this bell has just left a completed six. This is confirmed by noticing that, in this same change, the fourth bell enters into a new six. Hence *a parting of the sixes* has occurred between the second and third changes. It only remains, therefore, to discover whether the first and second changes form the end of a quick or a slow six. One way of doing this is by noticing the full leads, whether hand-and-back, as in a quick six, or back-and-hand, as in a slow one. Now all Grandsire ringers know that they bring their bells to lead at hand, hence the first and second changes of Stedman's " go off " are the fifth and sixth of a quick six.

We may now—seeing that the treble has gone up into the double-dodging hunt, and the fourth has come down therefrom, giving us 32415—proceed to prick a *slow* six,

taking 324 as representing 132, the first change in the previous
example. The result of this, together with the double
dodging behind, gives us 34251, as the last change of this
slow six. We are now, therefore, at another parting of the
sixes, and, as the last was a slow six, this must be a quick
one. We are compelled to pass the second out and let the
fifth in, and also to change the bells at the lead, so that a
whole pull *right* may be led ; this, therefore gives us 43521 as
the opening of the *quick* six. If we now take 435 as representing 213, the first change of the foregoing quick six example,
and complete the six, as well as the double dodging, we
shall get 34512 as the quick six end. If we now continue
· to prick slow and quick sixes, alternately, we shall find that
at the fourth change after the tenth six end (counting the
second change as the first six end) the bells come into rounds.
This, then, is the plain course of Stedman's Doubles.

An examination of the work of the bells behind shows
that a bell, after leaving the sixes, dodges twice on the way
up and then lies full, wrong (back-and-hand), after which it
dodges twice on the way down and again enters the sixes.

Now notice the paths of the two bells that first enter
the sixes ; the first of these, the fourth, remains therein during
five sixes ; whilst the next, the fifth, comes out again at once.
A further inspection shows that this rapid work falls to the
lot of the fourth the next time it enters the sixes ; and also
that the fifth, at its next turn, stays in five sixes. A still
further examination shows that in this plain course each bell,
including the treble, has a path, which, if we take the fourth
as an example, can be expressed thus, for Doubles :—

In front, five sixes.
Behind, two sixes.
In front, one six.
Behind, two sixes.

It may be noted that, when the fourth is behind, at the plain course end, it only gets a chance of working in four changes ; the missing two, to complete the six, will be found in the "go off."

Noting that the work done by a bell behind is *the same* on both occasions, it becomes necessary to learn the paths in which bells work when in the sixes. In connection with these, and the different sixes, there are certain technical terms which I will first explain. When a six, such as the first complete one in the plain course, has a bell that goes in and stays in, it is called "*a slow six.*" The bell that thus enters the sixes is said to "*go in slow,*" and the work it does, during the five sixes in which it is in front, is called the "*slow work.*" On leaving the sixes it is said to "*come out slow.*" When a bell, such as the fifth in the second six, goes into the six, hunts straight down to lead, and then hunts up and passes out of the six, it is said to "*go in quick,*" and the "*come out quick,*" and the six (every alternate one) in which this occurs is called a "*quick six.*"

If the path of a bell in the slow work be examined it will be seen that, after the middle of the third six, the work is merely reversed. Now this is noteworthy, and calls attention to the fact that certain parts of the slow work are relatively alike. These portions are usually described thus :—

First whole turn.
First half turn.
Last half turn.
Last whole turn.

The skeleton diagram—in which the hand-and-back strokes are coupled by the small brackets on the right—shows the different portions of the work to which these names refer. In learning this work care must be taken also to note at which stroke the different blows at the lead are struck, and how the third's are made, whether right or wrong.

When a bell comes in slow it makes third's, right (hand-and back), works down and leads full, wrong (back-and-hand), permits another bell to snap, and leads full, right; this is called the "*first whole turn.*" Working up, making third's wrong; working down, and snapping at hand, is comprised in the "*first half turn.*" This same again, with the third" right, and the snap at back, is the "*last half turn.*" Working up, making third's wrong; working down and leading full, right; permitting a snap, and leading full, wrong (similar work to the first whole turn), completes the "*last whole turn.*" After this you work up, make third's right, and leave the sixes.

In a plain course there are sixty changes; if a single be called, by which means two

First whole turn	0 0 4 0 0 0 0 4 0 0 0 4 0 0 0 4 0 0 0 0 4 0 0 0 0 0 4 0 0 0 4 0 0 0 0 4 0 0 0 0
First half turn	0 4 0 0 0 0 0 4 0 0 0 0 4 0 0 0 4 0 0 0 4 0 0 0 0
Last half turn	0 4 0 0 0 0 0 4 0 0 0 0 4 0 0 0 4 0 0 0 4 0 0 0 0
Last whole turn	0 4 0 0 0 0 0 4 0 0 0 0 4 0 0 0 4 0 0 0 4 0 0 0 0 4 0 0 0 0
Third's and out	0 4 0 0 0 4 0 0 0 0 4 0 0 0 0 0 4 0 0 0 0 0 4 0 0 0 0 4 0 0

bells are reversed, another course, with another single, will complete the peal.

In all Stedman ringing the mode of making bobs or singles is such that the work of the bells in the sixes is not interfered with ; in other words, the calls are always " *made* " by the bells behind.

At a single in Stedman's Doubles (diagram p. 40) the bell that comes out behind, after striking an odd blow there, *makes fourth place*, right, strikes another blow behind, and goes in again. The bell that has lain full, wrong, at the parting of the sixes, strikes an odd blow in fourth's, *lies full right*, strikes another blow in fourth's, and then lies full again, wrong, at the parting of the sixes, after which it commences to dodge in 4-5 down.*

At a single the two bells behind, in this way, change places with one another. It must, therefore, be remembered on again entering the sixes that their work is reversed ; that is, if a bell has come out quick, it will go in quick, instead of, as usual, going in slow ; or, if out slow, then in slow.

In dealing with Stedman's Triples instructions are given for ascertaining how a bell has to go in ; and as these explanations apply, partially, to Stedman on any number of bells, they should be here referred to (p. 27, etc.).

---

* As certain of my readers may visit towers in which Stedman's Doubles are rung with a different single to the one I have just explained, I would here observe that several writers have fallen into error in their descriptions of the single on this number of bells. Although two bells are reversed by the single they explain, it is not done in the customary and most symmetrical manner.

STEDMAN'S TRIPLES ; *Diagram p. 23.*

This method on seven differs from that on five by having two more dodging places. Thus, after double dodging in 4-5-up, each bell double dodges in 6-7 up, lies full, wrong, double dodges in 6-7 and 4-5 down, and then goes in, quick, or slow, as required. As the work in the sixes is exactly the same as in Doubles, my previous explanations stand good.

Bobs and singles in Stedman's Triples are made thus :—

	Bob :		Single :
	3 2 4 1 6 5 7		3 2 4 1 6 5 7
	2 3 4 6 1 7 5		2 3 4 6 1 7 5
	2 4 3 1 6 5 7		2 4 3 1 6 5 7
	4 2 3 6 1 7 5		4 2 3 6 1 7 5
	4 3 2 1 6 5 7		4 3 2 1 6 5 7
Bob {	3 4 2 6 1 7 5	Single {	3 4 2 6 1 7 5
{	4 3 6 2 1 5 7	{	4 3 6 2 1 7 5
	4 6 3 1 2 7 5		4 6 3 1 2 5 7
	6 4 3 2 1 5 7		6 4 3 2 1 7 5
	6 3 4 1 2 7 5		6 3 4 1 2 5 7
	3 6 4 2 1 5 7		3 6 4 2 1 7 5
	3 4 6 1 2 7 5		3 4 6 1 2 5 7

At a bob, the bell that has double dodged in 4-5 up makes fifth's place (wrong) at the parting of the sixes, and then double dodges in 4-5 down (this bell is said to make the bob) ; the bells behind continue dodging here through another six ; in other words, the five bells, in front, work as at a parting of the sixes in Doubles, whilst the two behind continue their dodging, and make in all five dodges.

At a single, the five bells, in front, work the same as at a bob ; but, of the two behind, one lies the whole pull as if no call had been made, whilst the other bell, namely, the one that has double dodged in 6-7 down, makes sixth's place, and then double dodges in 6-7 up, previous to again lying full.

When a bell is undisturbed in its work behind, in other words, if a bell leaves the sixes, and hunts up and down the double dodging places, without a call being made, it re-enters the sixes (quick or slow) in the contrary way to that in which it came out. If, however, calls are made, this re-entry may be altered, or not, according to circumstances, which we shall now set out.

First, it must be distinctly understood that in Stedman ringing, on any number of bells, it is the three hindermost only that are disturbed by a call; therefore, these only need their positions and work examining.

Neither a bob nor a single upsets the contrariwise re-entry of the bell that makes fifth's place; if such came out quick it will go in slow, and, *vice versa*, if out slow, then in quick. The reason for this will be clear to anyone who will notice that its work is altered by *two* sixes being missed out. Concerning the bells that have been dodging behind, and are forced to continue dodging; as these are delayed there for an entire six, it follows that if, in the usual course, one of them would have again entered the sixes as a slow bell, it will, now, not enter until the following six, which will, of course, be a quick one; and *vice versa*. Hence bells kept behind during a bob, or during any *uneven* number of consecutive bobs, instead of going in contrariwise as usual, will re-enter the same way they came out. When, however, two successive or any *even* number of successive bobs are called, the bells behind go in contrariwise as usual.

At a single, one bell lies the usual whole pull behind, and therefore goes in contrariwise. The bell that makes the sixth place continues behind during two extra sixes, and, therefore, also goes in contrariwise ; and the bell making fifths (in bob fashion) goes in contrariwise. Hence a single causes no alteration in the quick and slow work, all re-enter the sixes in the usual way, that is, contrariwise.

The foregoing rules necessitate a ringer's remembering how he came out—quick or slow. When three successive bobs are called, it is probable that any one unacquainted with the composition of the touch, or peal, may be in doubt as to whether two, three, or four have been called. I will, therefore, explain means by which a ringer may assure himself, before entering the sixes, whether he has to go in quick or slow. These aids require a ringer to carefully watch his course bell.

In ringing Stedman, especially on the higher numbers, the use of the course bell becomes a necessity, in order to find the bells to strike over when in the double dodging. Your course bell is that in the next higher dodging place, on the way up, and consequently in the next lower dodging place on the way down. Each bell, therefore, is preceded by its course bell on the way up, dodging behind with it previous to lying full, and is preceded by it on the way down. Therefore when any bell goes into 4-5 down, its course bell enters the sixes.

Observe the bells behind in the first six in the plain course of triples ; they are the fifth and the seventh, and the latter is the course bell of the former. When the fifth dodges in 4-5 down, the seventh enters the sixes, and, going in slow, strikes two blows in third's place. The fifth, therefore, strikes its first blow in fourth's place over the seventh, and is therefore assured that his course bell has gone in slow ;

because, had it gone in quick, it would have struck in second's place when he first struck in fourth's. At the end of the six he (the ringer of the fifth bell) will, therefore, have to go in quick. Of this he will be still further assured when he strikes his last blow in fourth's, by its *not* being over his course bell, as it would have been were it coming out quick. The following rules are therefore to be depended on :

If your first blow in fourth's place be over your course bell, it has gone in slow, and you will therefore go in quick.

If you do *not* strike the first blow in fourth's place over your course bell, it has gone in quick, and you will therefore go in slow.

The foregoing rules apply to the observation of the course bell at the earliest point for ascertaining how it has gone in. If, however, you are careless, and fail to notice the commencement of the six, you must watch your course bell at the six end, for :

If you do *not* strike over your course bell for the *last* blow in fourth's, it is in slow, and you must go in quick.

If you do so strike it, it is coming out quick, and you therefore go in slow.

.In order to strike well, especially when ringing a heavy bell, it is necessary to know how you are to go in *before* completing the last dodge in 4-5. For this reason I recommend each one to assure himself *at the beginning of the six* how he has to go in, allowing the six end to further confirm it, and in no case to leave the matter in doubt to the last blow.

I would also draw attention to the fact that, when dodging in 4-5 up, or down, the three blows struck in fourth's place are over the three front bells respectively. In dodging in 4-5 down, this knowledge is of much advantage in connection with the course bell observations.

The foregoing course bell observations are applicable at

all times ; but each ringer must note when and where his course bell is altered by a call, and then carefully select his new one ; for instance, the bell that makes the bob courses down after the one with which she was dodging in 4-5 out when the call was given ; and this bob-making bell becomes the course bell of the one kept dodging behind after lying.

In concluding these observations on Stedman's Principle, I may say that too much time can hardly be spent in the examination of a course in this method. Numerous observations may be found which, in ringing, will prove of great assistance. A learner can thus study the different positions which the bells in the slow work occupy, and the relation that their work bears to his own, at any given point. He will thus learn to notice the partings of the sixes, and will further know whether the bell then coming in should be a quick or slow one. By this means he may save a peal if, when the time comes, he can speak with confidence and accuracy.

With a view to directing a learner's observations into a systematic channel, the following diagrams have been drawn up :—In this first, you are supposed to be ringing the bell marked **X**, and to have for your course bell one marked **Q**. The diagram begins with the six in while you are dodging in 4-5 down, and it is taken for granted that you here know that, if you at once strike over your course bell, it has gone in slow. However, as you do *not* thus strike her you are assured that you have to go in slow, and at once make observations accordingly, remembering that you will meet her coming out at the six end. All quick bells are represented by **Q**.

The description of each line of these diagrams is given (as far as possible), side by side.

Being now in 4-5, your first blow	B	A	Q		**X**
in fourth's is over a slow bell marked A, ...	B	Q	A	**X**	
(doing its last whole turn), whilst your next	Q	B	A		**X**
in fourth's is over another slow bell B	Q	A	B	**X**	
(which is doing its first half turn), and	A	Q	B		**X**
your last over your quick course bell Q.	A	B	Q	**X**	
You now enter the sixes by making	B	A	**X**	Q	
third's place, right, over A and B;	A	B	**X**		
take A (about to make his " thirds and out ")	A	**X**	B		
and dismiss him from your mind, and	**X**	A	B		
then lead full, wrong, looking out for	**X**	B	A		
B who will snap and leave you to	B	**X**	A	Q	
lead full right. This opens a quick six, ...	**X**	B	Q	A	
and ends your first whole turn.	**X**	Q	B		
Q, a quick bell, now leads and B	Q	**X**	B		
follows (in quick-six-end style) whilst you	Q	B	**X**		
make thirds, wrong, over B and Q; you	B	Q	**X**		
then open a slow-six by snapping at hand	B	**X**	Q	C	
from B, *and complete your first half turn.*	**X**	B	C	Q	
Leaving B to complete her last whole	B	**X**	C		
turn, watch for C, the new slow bell, and	B	C	**X**		
make thirds, right, over her and B; B	C	B	**X**		
makes " thirds and out," *and you complete your*	C	**X**	B		
last half turn by snapping at back from C.	**X**	C	B	Q	
Leaving C to open the quick six and	C	**X**	Q	B	
complete her first half turn, strike over	C	Q	**X**		
Q and C for your third's wrong. Now	Q	C	**X**		
take Q again, *remembering that she will*	Q	**X**	C		
be your course bell out, and then lead	**X**	Q	C		
full, right, and close the six. C now	**X**	C	Q	D	
snaps (completing her first half turn)	C	**X**	D	Q	
and you finish your last whole turn by	**X**	C	D		
leading full, wrong.	**X**	D	C		
Note the new slow bell D as you	D	**X**	C		
pass her, and make thirds, right, over C	D	C	**X**		
and this slow bell.	C	D	**X**	Q	
You then leave the sixes by letting a quick	D	C	Q	**X**	
bell enter (this bell will course you out).	D	Q	C		**X**
Here in 4-5, you again meet the bells over	Q	D	C	**X**	
which you made your " thirds and out," first	Q	C	D		**X**
C and then D, and this ends your dealings	C	Q	D	**X**	
with the bells in front.	C	D	Q		**X**

In looking over this diagram there is much for a learner
to note. For instance, you make five third's places ; one as
you enter, one as you leave, and one in the exact centre of
your slow work, and these three, falling in slow sixes, are
made right (that is hand-and-back) ; the other two fall in
the intermediate quick sixes, and therefore come wrong (back-
and-hand). Quick bells lead full in quick sixes, of course,
and therefore lead right, and their leads are preceded and
followed by full leads, right, by bells doing whole-turn work.
The slow sixes begin and end with snaps, and all other leads
are full, wrong.

It is, again, worth while noticing with what regularity
(leads excepted) you work with the others in front ; for
instance, **A** and **B** are struck in 4-5 down : again, over
A and **B** third's are made ; **A** is then taken and **B** allowed
to snap, and so you get through your first whole turn. The
quick six is got through by taking, twice, the quick bell
and **B** (**Q** & **B** and **Q** & **B**), and this brings you to the end of
your first half turn. Your last half turn (or, in other words,
the work of your central six, which is a slow one), may be
summed up thus : Take **B** and **C,** twice (**B** & **C** and **B** & **C**),
C being the new slow bell. The quick six commencing your
last whole turn may be put this : Take **C** and **Q** twice
(**C** & **Q** and **C** & **Q**) ; afterwards let **C** snap, and take **D** (the
last of the slow bells), make third's over **C** and **D,** and again
strike **C** and **D** when dodging in 4-5 out.

Referring to the four snap leads ; the first snapped from
you is by a bell **B** doing its last half turn ; the second, snapped
by you is from the same bell now doing its last whole turn ;
the third, snapped by you, when doing your last half turn,

is from a bell **C** doing its first whole turn ; and the fourth and last, snapped from you when doing your last whole turn, is by the same bell **C** now doing its first half turn. Thus you give and take from **B,** and then take and give to **C**.

In this second diagram, which begins and ends with the double dodging in 4-5, you are supposed to be ringing the bell marked **Q,** and to have been coursing **B** down.

If, in stepping down into 4-5, you immediately strike over your course bell, you know that he has gone in slow, and that you will have to go in quick.

Here you do so strike her ; hence your dealings with the bells in front are as follows :

	Your first blow in fourth's is	......	A	S	B		Q
B	over your course bell B :	......	S	A	B	Q	
	Your next is over a slow bell	.. ...	S	B	A		Q
A	doing its last half turn, marked A :	......	B	S	A	Q	
	Your last is over an outgoing	......	B	A	S		Q
S	slow bell S (*your course bell out*).	......	A	B	S	Q	
A	You now take A again, and	....	B	A	Q		
B	once more your course bell B :	......	B	Q	A		
	and lead	....	Q	B	A		
	full, right :	......	Q	A	B		
A	Begin again with A.	......	A	Q	B		
B	again take your course bell B,	......	A	B	Q		
S	and admit another slow bell, S,	......	B	A	S	Q	
	into the sixes.	......	A	B	S		Q
B	Once more take B your	......	A	S	B	Q	
	course bell, and finish	...	S	A	B		Q
A	by again striking over A.	......	S	B	A	Q	
			B	S	A		Q

The letters on the left hand of the lines are intended to show at a glance the order in which the bells are taken. The last blow before entering the sixes is over a slow bell **S,** and the first after leaving them is over another slow bell **S.** Now, the first **S** may be taken as " sandwiched " between **A** and **A**, with outside crusts formed by the course bell **B** and **B.** The second **S** is likewise " sandwiched," but between the course bell **B** and **B,** with the outsides formed by **A** and **A.** It is as well to distinguish your course bell as your *course bell*, and to think of **A** as standing for *another.* Then the whole of your work lies with your course bell and another, with the exception only of the slow bells you allow to pass out and in.

There is another observation, for the introduction of which an apology is almost necessary, as it is undoubtedly one which should never be used except as a last resource, since no one using it can strike well. It is this : On going into the sixes, and when striking your first blow (in third's) notice the two bells, say **B** and **A** in front (see previous diagrams). Having struck over the last of these two, say **A,** you proceed—regardless of consequences—to strike your next blow over the other bell, **B.** If **B** proves to have been leading full, your second blow will have been in second's place (or an apology for it), and you are a quick bell. If, however, whilst striking after **B** you find yourself kept back in third's, by **A** stepping in front of **B,** you are a slow bell.

One more remark before closing this chapter. If ever, in dodging in 4-5 up, after leaving the sixes, you meet with a wavering companion whose face tells you he is in doubt, direct him into the sixes in the *same* way you passed through them. This hint is often most opportune, more especially if the bells are having a rough time of it in front ; it is easily given, and a glance at the diagram will fix it on your mind.

(For further information see " Stedman " of this Series.)

CHAP. V.—PLAIN METHODS ON FIVE BELLS.

Diagram page 1.

In the following methods the treble has a plain hunting course. Before attempting to learn the duty of a bell, the different points at which places are made should be considered. I shall therefore first call attention to the place-making, and then specify the details of the duty. The reader must understand that I shall not treat the whole pulls at the lead, or at the back, as places. For the sake of brevity, I shall use the words "*lead*" and "*lie*," instead of lead a whole pull, or lie a whole pull behind; and when "*snaps*" (single "run-a-way" blows) occur, I shall specially mention them.

St. Simon's Doubles.

(Dates from Stedman's time, substantially, as "Church Doubles.")

When the treble is above third's, or behind, as it is called (in other words, after the treble hunts up from third's place, until it returns there, on the way down), third's places are made; when the treble leads, second's place is made.

The two third's places that are made, when the treble is behind, cause the bells in front to make a double dodge. When the treble leads, the bells work as in Plain Bob. Each bell, after leaving the lead, does not return there until it has completed the intermediate duty of the course. This is expressed by saying that the duty is "*continuous.*" In these cases it is best to learn the duty in a single lesson, thus .

St. Simon's Doubles. Duty of a bell after making second's place.

Lead and double dodge after; and dodge in 3-4 up.

Lie; third's and up to lie four blows; third's and up to lie.

Dodge in 3-4 down; double dodge before leading; and make second's place.

This lesson may be shortened if the work at the lead be treated as a distinct part. Suppose we class it as " *work at the lead* "; we can then learn the duty of a bell after leaving the lead, and end the lesson with " work at the lead," which latter would run thus : Double dodge before leading, second's place, lead and double dodge after.

Bob.—At a bob, fourth's place, instead of second's place. is made. The work of the bell that lies four blows behind is not altered ; that of the others is altered as follows

St. Simon's Doubles. A Bob alters the work of the bells thus :

A bell, that has just completed the work in front, instead of dodging in 3-4, makes fourth's place, and goes down again to the work in front.

A bell, that would have made second's place, runs out quick, lies. and then makes the first third's place of the duty behind.

A bell, that would have dodged in 3-4 down, runs in quick, leads. and takes up the remainder of the work in front.

NEW DOUBLES.

(Dates from Stedman's time)

The place-making is the same as in St. Simon's Doubles when the treble is behind, but third's places are also made when the treble is in front, as well as second's place. The duty may be learnt in one continuous lesson as before.

The work is front is exactly the same at St. Simon's. On leaving this you make third's place, instead of dodging in 3-4. On arriving at the back you " *snap* " there, at hand stroke, and make another third's place. You then hunt up and lie, wrong (back-and-hand stroke) ; lie, right ; and again lie, wrong ; permitting snaps between. The treble then turns you from behind and you make third's place, returning to snap another blow behind, this time at back stroke. Another third's place is made, in hunting down to lead, where you take up the front work. This duty may be tabulated thus :

New Doubles. Duty of a bell after leaving the work in front.

Third's place, snap behind at hand, third's place and up.

Lie, wrong ; lie, right ; and lie, wrong (permitting snaps between).

Third's place, snap behind at back-stroke, third's place, and down to the work in front.

Bob.—At a bob, fourth's place, instead of second's place, is made ; the work of the bell behind is not altered ; that of the others is altered as follows :

New Doubles. A Bob alters the work of the bells thus : *

A bell, that has just snapped at back-stroke, makes fourth's place, snaps at hand and commences the work behind again.

A bell, that would have made second's place, makes third's place, and commences the work in front again.

A bell, that has just made third's after completing the work in front, goes down again, and takes up the remainder of the front works

STEDMAN'S SLOW COURSE.*

(First given in the " Clavis," 1788, in Minor form ; adapted to Doubles by Shipway, 1816).

In this the bells make places when the treble is behind them. For this reason, when hunting up, the path of each bell, after passing the treble, is always a plain hunt until the treble is again taken on the way down. Two third's places are made when the treble is behind ; and, when she is lying there, second's place is also made. This causes the work of a bell in front (see the first lead) to be the reverse of that behind in New Doubles. The duty is not continuous. Each bell arrives twice at the lead, and on each occasion does

* Introduced here for the sake of variety, although somewhat irregular.

different work ; and twice at the back, when, however, the same work is done. The different work in front may be classed as the " *long* " and " *short* " work ; and as these are separated by the " *work behind,*" the whole may be tabulated thus :

Long work in front.—Lead, right : lead, wrong ; lead, right (permitting snaps between) ; and hunt up.

Work behind.—Lie ; third's place ; lie and down.

Short work in front.—Snap at hand ; make second's place, wrong , snap at back ; and hunt up.

This work may now be summarised, so as to give the duty in a course as follows :

Stedman's Slow Course. Duty of a bell after turning the treble from the lead.

Long work in front, first work behind.
Short work in front, second work behind.

It is always easy to tell on arriving at the front which work has to be done ; because it is only when a bell turns the treble from the lead that the long work has to be done.

Bob.—Unfortunately a bob has to be made in a very " lop-sided " way ; first third's only, as annexed, is made ; the bell that has just completed the long duty in front remains unaltered ; the others are altered as follows :

```
2 1 4 5 3
1 2 4 3 5
1 4 2 5 3
4 1 5 2 3
4 5 1 3 2
5 4 3 1 2
```

Stedman's Slow Course. A bob alters the work of the bells thus :

A bell, that has done the short work in front, makes third's and goes down to the long work in front.

A bell, that is finishing the first work behind, instead of lying, dodges in 4-5, and then commences the second work behind.

A bell, that has just completed the second duty behind, dodges in 4-5, and hunts down to the short work in front.

CARTER'S PRINCIPLE.

DOUBLES ON CARTER'S PRINCIPLE.   (*Diagram page* 41).

The introduction of another diagram for five-bell ringers, which Mr. John Carter worked out in 1893, calls for no apology, as it is sure to be appreciated by those for whom it is intended, namely, the experts.

It will, perhaps, not prove quite as difficult as it looks : for, if the diagram be examined, the points marked (*) will be seen to be centres, round which the paths of the bells reverse themselves.

The duty in Doubles may be described thus :
Front work.
First whole-turn, at the back.
Snapping work, in the order of, Front, Back, and Front.
Second whole-turn, at the back.

The front work comprises a dodge behind in 4-5, a quick run in, a double dodge on the lead, three full leads separated by two snaps, another double dodge, and a quick run out to the dodge behind in 4-5.

In proceeding to a snap, and in retiring from one, whether at the lead or at the back, a third's place is invariably made.

If these specified points be studied, and then carefully connected in the learner's mind by aid of the diagram, a plain course should present no difficulty with five good men.

Single.—Two bells change places at a single, namely :

(*a*) The bell that (after its snapping work) has done its whole-turn behind, proceeds to make fourth's place, and goes behind again for another whole-turn, previous to recommencing its snapping work.

(*b*) The bell that, after its front work, has run out quick, lies full, and runs in quick again to the front.

Triples.—In triples, etc., Bobs and Singles are made by the three bells behind, as in Stedman, across the lines of division, be they " Fours " or " Eights." The five-bell work in front remains the same, except so far as it is cut in two by bells going out to, and coming in from, the dodging work in 6-7. A few rows of Triples are annexed to make this plain. If the diagram of Doubles be examined with Triples in view, it will be seen that (1) the two paths set out in the two columns are both shown commenicng and ending with a whole pull behind, and (2) that this whole pull is situated across a dividing line; hence, here, in triples, etc., on two occasions a bell leaves the five bell work, and for two divisions (for triples) joins in dodging work behind. For example :

1	2	3	4	5	6	7
2	1	4	3	6	5	7
1	2	4	6	3	7	5
1	4	2	3	6	5	7
4	1	2	6	3	7	5
1	4	6	2	7	3	5
1	6	4	7	2	5	3
6	1	4	2	7	3	5
1	6	2	4	7	5	3
6	1	2	7	4	3	5
1	6	7	2	4	5	3
6	1	7	4	2	3	5
6	7	1	2	4	5	3
7	6	2	1	5	4	3
6	7	2	5	1	3	4
6	2	7	1	5	4	3
2	6	7	5	1	3	4
6	2	5	7	3	1	4
6	5	2	3	7	4	1
5	6	2	7	3	1	4
6	5	7	2	3	4	1
5	6	7	3	2	1	4
6	5	3	7	2	4	1
5	6	3	2	7	1	4
5	3	6	7	2	4	1
3	5	7	6	4	2	1

A bell that is running out, quick, dodges in 4-5 (as in Doubles), and, passing out, triple dodges in 6-7; lies, and makes a solitary dodge *after*. It then dodges in 4-5 down and makes fifth's (a remant of the whole-turn behind in Doubles), and, as it is now about to take up its snapping work, it also makes third's on the way down to snap at the lead.

Alternately, when the same, or any other, bell leaves the snapping work, it makes fifth's, dodges in 4-5, and dodges (once) in 6-7, before lying; after which it makes a triple dodge, goes down into 4-5, where it dodges, and runs in quick to begin the front work again.

At first it might appear difficult to know whether to go down for front-work or for snapping-work, but the uneven dodging behind settles this; and it ought not to be difficult for the bell that is lying behind to keep the new comer right, and so on. Bobs and singles will, of course, increase the necessity of those behind keeping a sharp look-out, but what else does the keen ringer relish ?

Mr. Carter points out that what is here termed the snapping-work might equally be called the back-slow, as the bulk of the work is really at the back, the bell in question merely slipping down on two occasions " to see that the front work is all right." This is happily expressed, as trouble will certainly occur if a proper reception be not extended to the visitor !

CHAP. VI.—PLAIN METHODS ON SIX BELLS.

BEFORE proceeding to detailed descriptions, it is necessary to make a few remarks on the way in which the bobs and singles are made in these examples, as in some cases the mode of making the single hitherto adopted is open to objection.

In Double Court, for instance (diagram p. 3), at a plain lead sixth's place, and at a bob lead fourth's place, is made. Now Stedman, in his *Campanalogia*, published in 1677, and all subsequent writers, shew the singles to be made by the bells lying still in second's, third's, and sixth's places ; the object being, I suppose, to have the singles at the half-peal ends, without reversing the tenors. This plan, however, necessitates the making of two places such as have no counterpart at either plain or bob leads. My opinion is that *two* of the places made should be those made at plain and bob leads, leaving *one* new place only to be arranged. Thus one bell will make a plain lead place, one a bob place, and one the place between these two, leaving the two others unaltered in their plain lead work. In Double Court, therefore, as sixth's place is made at a plain lead, and fourth's place at a bob, I shew the single to be made in fourth's, fifth's, and sixth's places ; and in this way I have also treated College Single (diagram p. 4). Of course, in peals, in these methods, it will be necessary to have the singles at some place other than the half-peal ends, so that the tenors may not be reversed.

St. Clement's Bob *Diagram p. 2—(Appears in 1702, except that fourth's place, instead of second's, was made, the resulting lead-ends being irregular).*

In this method third's places are made whenever the treble is above that place ; whilst, when she is at the lead, second's place is made, and the other bells dodge as in Plain Bob ; in fact, the method would seem to be an extension of St. Simon's Doubles.

St. Clement's.   Duty of each bell after making second's place.

1.—Lead, triple dodge after, and dodge in 3-4 up.
2.—Lie, third's, pass treble in 3-4, and dodge behind (before lying).
3.—Lie, third's, pass treble in 4-5, lie and dodge after.
4.—Third's, pass treble in 5-6, lie, dodge in 3-4 down, and make
5.—triple dodge before leading.

Bob.—The Bob is that of Bob Minor, the alterations of duty being as follows :

The bell that would have dodged in 3-4 out, makes fourth's, and goes down again to the triple dodge.

The bell that would have made second's runs out quick ; afterwards making third's, and passing the treble in 3-4.

The bell that would have dodged in 3-4 down, runs in quick, and leads, prior to its triple dodge.

Single.—The Single is that of Bob Minor. At a single, second's place is made as at a plain lead ; fourth's place, as at a bob ; and third's place is made by the bell that would otherwise have dodged in 3-4 down, after which it returns behind, and begins the third's places again.

DOUBLE COURT : *Diagram page* 3.

(Dates from Stedman's time.)

In this, third's and fourth's places are made, before the treble leads ; and fourth's and third's places, after it has led. A bell, after making either set of places, continues in the direction in which it was previously hunting.

Special attention must be directed to the work of the bells which come to the front, or go behind, between the visits of the treble. This work, both in front and behind, is confined to three bells. One bell, turning the treble away, leads and then dodges ; one dodges both before and after leading ; and the other dodges and then leads, being turned away by the treble. In a similar manner three bells work behind. Were it necessary to describe the different parts of the work, I should refer to the bells which dodge both before and after leading, and lying, as those doing the " *full work* " ; but the work to be done in front and behind, can be so readily ascertained by observing the treble, that further terms are needless. For instance, if, on going down to lead, *you do not turn the treble away*, you dodge and then lead, after which, *if the treble does not turn you away*, you make another dodge ; in other words, always dodge before and after leading, if the treble does not prevent you. By observing the treble behind in the same way the duty there may be ascertained.

After obtaining a thorough knowledge of the work in front, and behind, the remaining duty in the course, which consists of the place-making, will be found very simple. Except when place making, each bell hunts straight up and down. The bells *turned from the lead, or from behind, by the treble,* are those which have to make the places. Thus, if the treble turns you from the front, you make fourth's, and third's, on the way up ; and if the treble turns you from behind, you make third's and fourth's on the way down. This method is in fact so simple that each can ascertain his work as the ringing proceeds ; I shall not therefore give any rules for the order in which the different duties occur, as these are clearly shown by the diagram.

Bob.—At a bob, fourth's place, instead of sixth's place, is made ; the bells in front (the place-making bells) work as at a plain lead ; and the bells behind make a triple (three-pull) dodge, that is, they dodge until the treble comes up and separates them. The alterations may be summarised thus :

A bell, that has just completed the full work in front (and that passes the treble in 2-3), makes fourth's place, and goes down again

A bell, that turns the treble from behind, makes a triple dodge after lying.

A bell, that passes the treble in 4-5, makes a triple dodge before lying.

Single (see page 41).—At a single, fourth's, fifth's, and sixth's places are made. The bell that turns the treble from behind lies and dodges ; makes fifth's place ; and then dodges and lies again. This bell is turned from behind by the treble, and consequently becomes a place-making bell.

DOUBLE OXFORD ; *Diagram page* 3.

(Dates from Stedman's time.)

The places made are the same as in Double Court, with the addition of second's and fifth's, made respectively when the treble leads, and lies. These additional places compel a bell to complete the work in front, or behind, at one visit ; that is, each bell on coming to the front, or on going behind, makes a triple dodge ; leads, or lies ; makes second's, or fifth's place, as the case may be ; then leads, or lies, and then makes another triple dodge. The other places are made by .the bells as they pass to and from the lead. Thus, on the way up, fourth's and third's are made, and on the way down, third's and fourth's ; each bell also dodges in 3-4, both before and after making these places. The work, which is continuous, can therefore be classified thus :

Double Oxford. Duty of each bell in a plain course.

Work in front. Place-making going up.
Work behind. Place-making coming down.

Bob.—At a bob, fourth's place, instead of second's, is made ; the bells behind (those making the triple dodge) work as at a plain lead ; the others are altered as follows :

A bell, that has just completed the work in front, makes fourth's place, at once, and then hunts down and begins the work in front again.

A bell, that would have made second's place, runs out, makes fourth's and third's, and so on, up to the back.

A bell, after making fourth's, on the way down, runs in, turns the treble from the lead, and completes the remainder of the work in front.

Single.—At a single, second's, third's, and fourth's places are made. The bell that has just made fourth's place on the way down, makes *third's place ;* then fourth's and third's places, and so on, up to the back.

COLLEGE SINGLE REVERSE ; *Diagram page* 4.

(Dates from Stedman's time, substantially, as College Little Bob).

The principle of this method consists in each one making third's place, on his way down, when the treble is above him. This causes you, when in front, to make a triple dodge after, or before, leading. It is practically St. Clements' Bob. with sixth's place made when the treble leads, instead of second's.

The simplest way to learn the work is by noticing that, if, in hunting down, you meet the treble when she is above third's, you make third's place and return behind. The bell that *cuts* the treble in 3-2 makes a triple dodge, *before* leading. and the bell that turns the treble from the lead makes a triple dodge *after* leading.

Bob.—A bob is made, as in Double Court, by making fourth's instead of sixth's place.

The bell that has left the front, with a triple dodge, makes fourth's place, and goes down to another triple dodge.

The bell that passes the treble in 3-4 (after third's) dodges *before* lying.

The bell that passes the treble in 4-5 (after third's) dodges *after* lying.

Single.—At a single the " bob bell " does not deviate from its work. The bell that passes the treble in 4-5 makes fifth's place (that is " makes the single "), and returns behind. The bell that passes the treble in 3-4 behaves as at a plain lead, that is, lies behind.

CANTERBURY PLEASURE ; *Diagram page* 4.

In this method, which is believed to be a comparatively modern one, " Imperial " places are made—when the treble is behind—by the working bells passing through third's and fourth's. At the treble's lead sixth's place is made, and fifth's when she lies behind.

Duty of a bell after its work behind with the treble.

1.—Lead, third's and fourth's, wrong, on the way out, and lie
2.—Cut the treble in 3-2, and lead and dodge, pass her in 3-4, and lie.
3.—Cut the treble in 4-3 and dodge before leading, passing her in 2-3 on the way out.
4.—After lying, make third's and fourth's (wrong), lead, and pass the treble in 2-3.
5.—Make fifth's between your whole pulls behind.

Bob.—The bob is made as in Double Court.

The bell that passes the treble in 2-3 makes the bob, that is, makes fourth's, and returns to lead and dodge.

The bells that, respectively, pass the treble in 4-5 and 3-4 dodge behind *after* and *before* lying.

Single.—The bell that " makes the single " is that which makes the places on the way out, and lies, she then makes fifth's, lies, and again makes the places on the way down.

DOUBLE BOB ; *Diagram page 5.*

(Dates from Stedman's time)

In this, fifth's place is made when the treble lies, as well as second's place when she leads. Besides the usual Plain Bob work, there is, therefore, dodging in 1-2, and 3-4, when the treble is behind.

The simplest way to learn this method will be to take the extra duty in the order in which it occurs *after* the ordinary Plain Bob work when the treble is at the lead. It may be tabulated thus, in two columns :

Double Bob.　Duty of each bell in a plain course.

1-2 —Second's place　....Dodge in 3-4 up.

4-5.—Dodge in 5-6 down ..Dodge before leading.

2-3.—Dodge in 3-4 up ....Make fifth's place.

5-6.—Dodge in 3-4 down ..Dodge after leading.

3-4.—Dodge in 5-6 up . ..Dodge in 3-4 down.

In these rules no mention is made of the ordinary detail duty, which, however, must be thoroughly understood. For instance, after passing the treble in 2-3, you dodge in 3-4 up, and lie ; the treble then turns you from behind, so you make fifth's place, and go behind again. This causes you to pass the treble in 5-6 ; and makes you dodge in 3-4 down ; and so on.

Bobs and Singles.—The bobs and singles are made when the treble leads, and are the same as those in Plain Bob.

CHAP. VII.—TREBLE BOB METHODS ON SIX BELLS.

As the beginner is now leaving behind him the grand simplicity of Oxford and Kent, it cannot but be instructive to survey one or two of the main features of the place-making of the next seven peals, some of which, for intricacy, run the Surprise methods a very near race.

College Exercise, p. 11, has a leading feature that requires a bell leaving either the front or the back,—except when the treble is in the middle—to make the far and near places with a dodge inserted between them, which may be shortly set out thus :—" far—(dodge)—near "—after which the bell goes forward.

Westminster, p. 10, has a somewhat similar feature, for, on leaving the slow, " far—(dodge)—near " opens the place-making, linked together with " far—(dodge treble)—near," with an added dodge, after which the bell goes forward. On the way to the front this work is, of course, taken in a reverse order, which, whilst calling for attention, is not difficult, especially if it be remembered that the added dodge comes first.

Tulip, p. 12, demands a simple re-arrangement. viz.: " far—near—(dodge treble) " and forward ; and, reversely, on the way down—(dodge treble)—far—near.

Old Oxford, and College Bob IV., *pp.* 8 *and* 9, both have a bell that runs out of the slow into a 3-4 dodge with the treble, so we get—" (dodge treble)-far-near," & " (dodge)-far " and (back to the) " near " front. And, later—" far-(dodge)-near," & " far-(dodge treble)," and (back to the) " near " front (slow work).

Southwark, p. 13, has a place that may be remembered as " (dodge treble)-fourth's " ; and this, on the way down, becomes " fourth's-(dodge treble)."

Kentish Delight, p. 14, has a place that may be written thus :—" third's-(dodge treble)," and on the way down— " (dodge treble)-third's."

The best possible plan for obtaining a full grasp of these, and other places—whether solitary or linked together —is to study and trace the various places on the diagrams, in their relationship to the treble's path, and thus get a full knowledge of the obstructions—places—which compel you to take the work in any particular order, and, further, learn why you reverse that order on other occasions. The double stars (**) inserted in the " Duty of a Bell," denote, in all cases, the central turning-point where the path of the bell reverses itself.

If a learner will but study the places in which, and by which, he has to steer his course, he will soon discover a pathway infinitely superior to any mere string of words, however accurate they may be, and however valuable to the beginner.

The first five methods have all their whole-pulls in " right " order (hand-and-back). but in Southwark and Kentish Delight—especially in the latter—there will be found a good sprinkling of whole pulls " wrong."

OLD OXFORD TREBLE BOB (Modernised).

The first half lead of this dates back to 1677, when it was known as Oxford Triple Bob ; and as Woodbine it was a familiar friend in the old edition of this work. The lead-ends, however, proved themselves irregular, and to secure those of Plain Bob, fifth's place is now made with the treble behind, and second's with her in front.

The " go off " places are those of Oxford, followed by another fourth's (Delight) place in the next rows ; the combined effect being curious :—The fifth's place forces a triple dodge in the middle, as well as a dodge at the lead, which latter divides the slow work between two bells. The fourth's (Delight) place compels—together with second's at the treble lead—a seven pull dodge behind, and as the fifth's place detains a bell behind, the duty of a bell is " continuous."

Old Oxford. *Duty of a bell in a plain course.*

1. Make *two* slow-second's, dodge & lead ,—place;, (dodge treble) far-near, & (dodge)-far, and back to " near "-front :—
2. Complete this " near " by leading ; triple dodge in 3-4 ; (pass treble 4-5), seven pull dodge behind :—
3. Complete seven-pull dodge work, *fifths,* and commence seven-pull dodge work *after ,*
4. Complete seven-pull dodge ; (cut treble 5-4), triple dodge in 3-4 ; lead ; (pass treble 2-3), places, far-(dodge)-near, &
5. far-(dodge treble) and back to " near " slow-work, in reverse order, and lie next the treble.

Bob.—At a bob fourth's place is made instead of second's :

The (treble-dodged) place-making bell continues to make far-near-far, etc., until the treble rejoins it.

The bell that has commenced the slow makes fourth's and down —see Column II. for its after proceedings.

The bell that has passed the treble in 2-3 makes fourth's, and down into the slow.

College Bob, IV., *dates from* 1677.

The " go off," the fourth's (Delight) place, and the first eight rows, are the same as Old Oxford ; but when the treble dodges behind adjacent third's and fourth's are made. Again, we have second's, and fifth's, next the treble. As the alterations in the place-making are produced when the treble is behind, it will not be surprising to note that the columns of this and the last diagram are the same at the head and foot.

College Bob IV.   Duty of a bell in a plain course.

1. After making one slow second's, lead & triple dodge, places, (dodge treble)-far-near, & (dodge)-far, and back to " near " front : -
2. Complete the " near " by leading ; far-(dodge)-near , (pass treble in 4-5) seven-pull dodge behind :—
3. Complete seven-pull dodge work,* fifths,* and commence seven-pull dodge work *after* .—
4. Complete seven-pull dodge ; (cut treble in 5-4) far-(dodge)-near , lead ; (pass treble in 2-3) places, far-(dodge)-near. &
5. far-(dodge treble). and back to " near " slow work, in reverse order. and lie next the table.

Bob.—At a bob, fourth's place, instead of second's, is made, the bells behaving exactly as at a bob in Old Oxford, just described.

WESTMINSTER BOB ; *Diagram page* 10.

The first half of the treble lead dates from 1677, as College Bob V., but fifth's was then made, and an irregular lead-end resulted. In 1702. third's place, with the treble behind, was introduced. and Plain-bob lead-ends were then secured. It is noteworthy that here, from Stedman's time, is handed down to us a method which has places made not only at the usual treble-bob places, but also at the cross-sections, as the treble passes through 2-3 and 4-5, as well as when she leads and lies, and some critics, short-sighted historically, have innocently imagined that this full array of places constitutes a " Surprise Peal " ! Space is too valuable to waste on arguments, especially when it is well known that not until nearly 100 years after did the word "Surprise" appear in connection with a method in any printed book, and then only with such a fine example as Cambridge, which, being a genuine Surprise, may be taken as a standard.†

The " go off " and the first seven rows are the same as Old Oxford, but the three central third's places (namely those when the treble, and the bells that work with her, lie behind) quite alter the aspect of the work, which again provides a " continuous " path.

Westminster. Duty of a bell in a plain course.

1   After making one slow second's, dodge & lead, dodge & second's, dodge & lead, (pass treble in 2-3) and make places, far-(dodge)-near, far-

2.   (dodge treble)-near & extra dodge; and out to the treble behind ; seven-pull dodge. *after* :—

3.   Complete the seven-pull dodge ; and (cutting treble in 3-4), dodge before and after making *third's,*, (pass treble in 4-5), and commence seven-pull dodge, *before* ;

4.   Complete this dodge ; dodge the treble behind ; and go down to the places, (extra dodge)-far-(dodge treble)-near, & far-(dodge)-near,

5   And down to take up the slow, in reverse order, and lie next the treble.

Bob.—At a bob, fourth's, instead of second's, is made, the bells behaving as at a bob in Old Oxford.

† Westminster, notwithstanding its complete number of places, excludes itself from the "Surprise" family by its excellence as an example of "Stagnation Bob," a term coined by the Editor to express a method, full of places, peculiar to the early days of change-ringing. In these pairs of bells remained too long in one locality and blocked the way, too long in front, too long in the middle, or too long behind. It will be noticed, in this connection, that in Westminster a bell requires the whole plain course in which to cross and re-cross, whereas in Cambridge Surprise we have six paths across, as in Oxford, and in London Surprise as many as eight such journeys across are made. It is the multiplicity of places, *and* the mode of arranging them, so that they neither block the paths of the active bells nor produce irregular leads, that constitutes a "Surprise" example—mere places (internal, of course) alone will not accomplish the object.

COLLEGE EXERCISE ; *Diagram page* 11.

This, which dates from 1702, was given in the former editions. In it adjacent third's and fourth's are made, when the treble dodges both at the front and back. When the treble leads, and lies, second's and fifth's, respectively, are made, and the bells then behind, or before, make a triple dodge. Except when the treble is met there, any bell going into the middle makes the far place, dodges, and makes the near, and hunts straight on ; the dodge with the treble and the place-making being now divided. The " go off " and the first nine rows are " Oxford," and it is interesting to note how the absence of the fourth's (Delight) places frees the method of the multiple dodging behind, to which the ancients seem to have been so much attached. Meeting the treble in 3-4 forms a connecting link between the sets of triple dodges.

College Exercise.   Duty of a bell in a plain course.

1. Make one slow second's, lead & triple dodge—as in C.B., IV —dodge treble 3-4, and triple dodge before lying :—
2. Lie & dodge , (cut treble 5-4), make places, " far-(dodge)-near " ; lead ; (treble in 2-3), places, " far-(dodge)-near," (treble in front) :—
3. Complete the " near " ; full work behind, making *fifth's* under treble ; make places, " far-(dodge)-near," (treble in front) :—
4. Complete the " near " ; lead ; makes places, " far-(dodge)-near ; " (treble in 4-5), and triple dodge after lying : —
5. Dodge treble in 3-4, and take up the other half of the slow, in the reverse order, lying next the treble.

Bob.—At a bob, the bell left behind by the treble makes " far-near-far " places (third's, fourth's, and third's), whilst the bells in front run in and out as at a Bob in Old Oxford.

TULIP (Modernised); *Diagram page* 12.

The first half lead˙ is exactly that known in 1702, but here, when the treble lies, a bell is made to lead full, which brings up regular lead-ends, without interfering with the quick runs for which the method is famous.

The places at the " go off " are third's and sixth's, and ordinary treble bob work follows as far as the treble's cross-section in 4-5 ; here a third's (Delight) place is made, and fourth's at the treble's dodgings behind. The eight positions, where a beginner may wonder whether he dodges first or last, will in a great measure settle themselves if he will remember that there is a dodge behind at the treble's lead (as well as a neighbouring one in 3-4), with two con-secutive whole pulls behind on each side of it. And, again, that before and after the treble's dodging lead there are the usual two consecutive full leads, as well as three consecutive full leads in the middle of the treble lead. These the learner should fully master on the diagram.

Tulip. Duty of a bell in a plain course.

1. After one slow second's, dodge & lead ; make places-far-near-(dodge treble) ; lie and dodge ;
2. In quick (cutting the treble in 3-2), lead & dodge ; out quick ; treble work ; third's & dodge ;
3. Lie and dodge ; in quick (cutting treble in 5-4), *lead* ; out quick (treble in 4-5), dodge & lie ; dodge in 3-4 &—
4. Third's ; treble work behind ; in quick ; dodge & lead ; out quick (treble in 2-3),
5. Dodge and lie ; places, (dodge treble)-far & near ; take up the slow work, in reverse order, and lie next the treble.

Bob.—The bob is made by a bell (left behind by the treble) making the far-near-far (third's, fourth's, third's) places. A bell leaving the slow runs out quick to lie and dodge, whilst the bell that passes the treble in 4-5 (to dodge and lie) proceeds to run in quick, and takes up the deserted slow work.

SOUTHWARK ; *Diagram page* 13.

The above name has been selected by the Editor because the method, which is taken from a Report by the Central Council, bases itself on London Surprise, and so deserves a London title. The first seven rows, and, of course, the corresponding close of the treble lead, embrace London places, and, what is more, produce the self-same rows in the self-same order. Indeed, the similarity is so grrat that the student will do well to analyse for himself the effect of the place-making between the treble's 4-5 intersections.

At the " go off " third's and sixth's, wrong, are made by these bells lying still, and in the next two rows the places are again the same. Then an overlapping fourth's (Delight) place is at once made ; and so on, as usual, until the treble's 4-5 intersection, when the London Surprise place is omitted in third's, and appears at the lead, in ordinary treble bob style. Again, features in common with London, are third's, with the treble behind, and second's, with her at the lead.

Southwark. Duty of a bell in a plain course.

1. After a slow second's, lead, and out quick to treble ; treble work & 5,6,6 ;
2. Third's ; 6,5,6 ; in quick (cutting treble in 5-4), dodge & lead ; " places ", (dodge treble) fourth's ; and lie :—
3. Third's , (cut treble in 3-2), lead ; far-*near*-far ; lead ; (pass treble in 2-3), third's ;
4. Lie ; " places ", fourth's (dodge treble) ; lead & dodge ; out quick (passing treble in 4-5) ; 6,5,6 ; third's ,
5. strike 6,6,5 & treble work ; in quick to slow work in reverse order, and lie next the treble.

Bob.—The bell left doing " treble work & 5,6,6," makes fourth's and out; the bell leaving the slow makes third's and out, and snaps 6,5,6; whilst the bell that has thus snapped previously comes down and makes third's, and enters the slow.

KENTISH DELIGHT. *Diagram page* 14.

As this has Kent's " go off," the Editor, who is again indebted to a Report of the Central Council, has given it the above name. Although the first seven lines are row for row the same as Kent, and as simple, therefore, as can be, the central portion of the lead is practically " surprise " work, and therefore makes a fitting close to this collection of simpler Minor-Methods. The quantity of wrong-handed pulls increases its difficulty, and any beginner who has mastered it need have no fear of the Surprise Methods. With the exception of fifth's with the treble behind, the third's (Delight) places, and the slow second's, all places, proper, are " wrong " handed.

Kentish Delight. Duty of a bell in a plain course.

1. After a slow second's, snap at lead ; double dodge & fourth's ; (pass treble 4-5), and treble work behind :—
2. Fourth's & third's (Kent's) ; (cut treble in 3-2), whole-turn, second's, & lead ; " places ", third's-(dodge treble) ; *treble work behind* ;
3. " Places ", (dodge treble), third's , lead, second's, & whole-turn ; (pass treble in 2-3), third's & fourth's (Kent's).
4. Treble work behind ; third's & double dodge ; snap at lead, slow second's, lead, dodge treble, and out :—
5. (Kent's), third's & fourth's; full treble work with *fifths[4] behind, (Kent's) fourth's and third's, and into the slow.

Bob.—The bob is exactly Kent's, the bells running in and out being unaltered. The bell passing the treble in 4-5 makes two extra dodges after the work behind; whilst the bell previously dodging the treble in the middle makes two extra dodges before her work behind.

CHAP. VIII.—SURPRISE MINOR METHODS.

A few words of introduction cannot be out of place here if addressed to the beginner, as for the first time—as we believe—a set of seven genuine Surprise methods has been brought together for the use of the would-be experts.

LONDON'S *Place-making.*—The beginner should first turn to the "place-making" of London, p. 16, noting that the term is applied to the places which are linked together with the treble.   Here, a bell about to meet the treble in the middle (whether from the front or the back), makes the near place, dodges with the treble, and makes the far place, which may be shortly written thus :—" near-(dodge treble)-far."   Moreover, he will find that these very places occur in Chester, and Canterbury ; and, indeed, that this piece of London is to be found in all seven examples, with additions, which we shall now point out.

Portions tagged on to LONDON'S *Place-making.*—Turning to York and Beverley, pp. 17 and 18, " third's & dodge " ·is added when a bell is going out ; whilst on the way down the added piece is taken first, thus—" dodge & third's." The reverse order on the way down is not hard to remember if we note that the added dodge takes place at the treble's lead.

Portions prefixed to LONDON's *Place-making.*—If we turn to Carlisle, p. 19, it will be seen that when a bell has just left the front " (dodge)-fourth's " commences the place-making ; whilst on the way down this addition takes the form of " fourth's-(dodge)," the added dodge taking place— in both cases—when the treble is lying behind.

Portions prefixed and tagged on to LONDON's *Place-making.* —An examination of Cambridge, p. 15, shows that the piece prefixed in Carlisle is exactly that prefixed here when a bell is going up ; moreover, the piece tagged on is the same, so that, in whichever direction a bell is proceeding, the places become " (dodge)-far-near-(dodge treble)-far-near-(dodge)." Cambridge, therefore, the oldest Surprise method, seems to have gathered together the different varieties of the coming places, and used them from the very outset as a whole.

The " wrong " places should be analysed by the student : they are not set out here as their enumeration might confuse the situation, but they should be carefully studied and mastered on the diagram.

CAMBRIDGE SURPRISE MINOR ; *Diagram page* 15.

This is the first Surprise peal ever printed ; it appeared in 1753 in the fourth edition of the J.D. & C.M. Campanalogia, and is worthy of great attention. There is here an entire absence of the " stagnation bob " element, the bells—no longer locked in pairs—moving in and out, from front to back, in a manner that is both a wonder and a " surprise " ; especially when compared with Westminster, which has the same complete number of places. Westminster lead-ends date from 1702, but its places come down from Stedman's time.

In regard to the places .—In the half lead, third's and fourth's, in consecutive steps, are made *twice* by the same bell ; with sixth's in the " go off " pair of rows. Add fifth's and second's, respectively, with the treble behind and before. and you have all that call for attention, as the slow-second's is always in evidence. In speaking of places in a Surprise Method, all places, proper, are internal ones, although for purposes of description we may have to speak of sixth's (as above), although it is *not* a place, being part of the hunting course.

Cambridge Surprise. Duty of a bell in a plain course.

1. After a slow second's & treble work , out quick (treble 4-5) to 6,5, & treble work ;
2. In quick (cut treble 3-2), lead & dodge ; places, (dodge)-far-near, (dodge treble)-far-near-(dodge) :—
3. Proceed to 6,5, & treble work, *fifth's,* treble work & 5-6 ; down to places ;
4. Places, dodge)-far-near, (dodge treble)-far-near-(dodge) ; dodge & lead ; out quick (treble 2-3) to :—
5. Treble work & 5-6 ; in quick ; take up slow work, in reverse order, and lie next the treble.

Bob.—At a bob the place-making bell makes fourth's ; and the two bells in front run in and out quick.

LONDON SURPRISE MINOR ; *Diagram page* 16.
(*Taken from the " Clavis,"* 1788).

Here the " go off " makes, with rounds, third's and sixth's ; after which third's and fourth's, in overlapping steps, are made *twice*, one bell appearing in each pair of places : this in the half lead. Regarding the full lead, fourth's and second's, respectively, are made with the treble behind and before. It is important to notice the characteristic feature of four consecutive full leads, and four consecutive fourth's, with the treble behind ; and the four consecutive bells that lie behind when she is in front, accompanied by four consecutive bells in third's. As nearly all whole pulls are " wrong," it may be well for the learner to search out those that are " right." Those in harmony with the treble are amongst these, of course ; the others worthy of notice are two third's, and two fourth's, which should be found on the diagram.

London Surprise Minor. Duty of a bell in a plain course.

1. After a slow second's, snap ;   ; treble work & 5,6,6 ; and down to :—

2. Third's ; out to 6,5,6 ; fourth's ; lead ; places, near-(dodge treble)-far ; lie, and down to :—

3. Third's (cut treble 3-2) ; whole turn, *third's,* whole turn ; (treble in 2-3), third's and out :—

4. Lie ; places, near-(dodge treble)-far ; lead ; fourth's ; (treble in 4-5) and 6,5,6 ; third's and :—

5. Out to 6,6,5 & treble work ; fourth's ; take up slow work, in reverse order, and lie next the treble.

Bob.—At a bob the " 5,6,6 " bell makes fourth's and back ; whilst the bells in front make third's in running in and out.

YORK SURPRISE MINOR ; *Diagram page* 17.

(*Taken from the " Clavis,"* 1788).

This is Cambridge, exactly, for the first eight rows, and, of course, for the corresponding rows at the end of the lead : the six rows, when the treble is behind, being London, place for place. This the learner should verify.

York Surprise Minor.   Duty of a bell in a plain course.

1. After London's slow ; treble's : treble work & 5,6 (instead of 5,6,6), and down to :— fourth

2. Places, (dodge)-far, near-(dodge treble)-far ; lead ; fourth's ; (treble 4-5), 6,5, & treble work ;

3. In quick to London's whole turn, *third's*, whole turn ; (treble 2-3), out quick to :—

4. Treble work & 5,6 ; fourth's ; lead ; places, near-(dodge treble)-far, near-(dodge) ;

5. Behind to 6,5, & treble work ; third's ; take up London's slow work, and lie next the treble. fourth

Bob.—A bob is made as in Cambridge—which see.

BEVERLEY SURPRISE MINOR ;   *Diagram page* 18.

This, for the first ten rows, and, of course, for the corresponding close of the lead, is York ; fifth's and second's are made with the treble behind and before ; with two curiously introduced consecutive third's with the treble behind, which makes a characteristic middle portion. It was pieced together by the Editor when experimenting, with a view to secure unblemished Surprise methods, and was given the name of Beverley as the sister Minster of York, whose foundation—speaking figuratively—it is built upon. In all probability it is an old friend, nevertheless.

Beverley Surprise Minor.   Duty of a bell in a plain course.

1. After London's slow work ; third's-fourth's-third's ; (treble 4-5), 6,5, & treble work ;

2. In quick : (cutting treble 3-2), whole turn & double dodge : places, near-(dodge treble)-far, near-(dodge) ;

3. Behind to 6,5, & treble work, *fifths,* treble work & 5,6 : and down to places-

4. (Dodge)-far, near, (dodge treble)-far ; double dodge & whole turn at lead : (treble in 2-3), out quick :—

5. Treble work & 5,6 ; (cut treble 5-4), fourth's-third's-fourth's ; take up London's slow, in reverse order, and lie next the treble.

Bob.—The treble-dodged place-making bell falls in fourth's place at the treble's lead ; whilst the bells in front run in and out quick.

CARLISLE SURPRISE MINOR ; *Diagram page* 19.

(Taken from the " Clavis," 1788.)

The " go off " of this (which is like London, except that third's and *fourth's* are made) is common also to Chester and Canterbury, all three methods having their first eight rows alike. Fifth's and second's, respectively, with the treble behind and before, are made, and a comparison with Cambridge will show the middle with the treble behind to be the same place for place. A peculiarity in the third's and fourth's, which occur twice in the half lead, is that one bell appears in three of these places.

The similarity of the first eight rows of these three methods (which, it will be noticed, all turn up '63 at back stroke twice in the first six rows) link them together, and, unfortunately, they each produce '65 at back stroke, twice in each part, and therefore not less than six times in the 720. When, however, the cramped positions, which are demanded in a method before it is admitted to be a Surprise example, are taken into account, there is reason to be thankful that we get four perfect examples with every one of the twenty-four '65 at hand-stroke. It is easy to avoid the '65 at part-ends and the like, but it is seemingly impossible to do so at all the internal positions.

Carlisle Surprise Minor.   Duty of a bell in a plain course.

1. After a slow second's & treble work—as in Cambridge ; run out quick (treble 4-5) to 6,5,6 ; and down to third's (part of third's-fourth's-third's) ;

2. Complete fourth's-third's (cut treble in 3-2), lead & dodge , places, dodge-far-near-(dodge treble)-far, and 6,5, &—

3. Treble work linked to treble work, *fifths,* treble work linked to treble work & 5,6 ,

4. Places, near-(dodge treble)-far, near-(dodge), and dodge before leading ; (treble in 2-3), third's-fourth's-third's ;

5. Out to 6,5,6 ; in quick to take up the slow, in reverse order, as in Cambridge, and lie next the treble.

Bob.—A bell passing the treble in 2-3 makes, as in Kent's bob, third's, double-fourth's, third's. and in ; the bells in front making thirds in running in and out—these are the bells doing " 6,5,6 " work.

Chester Surprise Minor ;   *Diagram page* 20.
(Taken from the " Clavis," 1788.)

After what has been said under Carlisle, we need only refer to the middle portion, where the treble is behind— fifth's (and second's), being again the same. An examination will show that it is the same as Beverley.

Chester Surprise.   Duty of a bell in a plain course.

1. After a slow second's, with snap (as in London), make fourth's-third's-fourth's , (treble in 4-5) 6,5,6 , and down to third's-fourth's-third's :—

2. Complete third's-fourth's-third's ; (cut treble in 3-2) ; whole turn & double dodge ; London places, near-(dodge treble)-far ; and 6,5 and—

3. Treble work linked to treble work, *fifths,* treble work linked to treble work & 5,6 .

4. Down to places, near-(dodge treble)-far ; double dodge at leads & whole turn ; (treble 2-3), third's-fourth's-third's :—

5. Out to 6,5,6, (cut treble 5-4), fourth's-third's-fourth's ; take up London's slow, and lie next the treble.

Bob.—The bell passing the treble in 2-3 makes, as in Carlisle, third's, double-fourth's, third's, and in; the bells in front making third's in running in and out, namely, the bells doing 6,5,6 work.

CANTERBURY SURPRISE MINOR; *Diagram page* 21.

Both the figures and the name are selected from the Central Council's publications.

Referring to the two previous examples, and to what we say of them, we need only call attention to the fourth's and second's, respectively, with the treble behind and before, and then point out that the six middle rows will prove to have the same places as London.

Canterbury Surprise. Duty of a bell in a plain course.

1. After a slow second's, with snap (as in London); make fourth's; treble work behind linked to treble work, & 5,6;

2. London places, near-(dodge treble)-far; lead; fourth's; (treble 4-5) 6,5,6, third's-fourth's-third's;

3. Complete third's-fourth's-third's (cut treble 3-2), *whole turn—(third's)—whole turn* (treble 2-3), third's-fourth's-third's;

4. Out to 6,5,6; (cut treble in 5-4) fourth's; lead; London places, near-(dodge treble)-far; 5,6,—

5. (5,6) and treble work linked to treble work; fourth's; down to take up London's slow work, and lie next the treble.

Bob.—At a bob, third's, double-fourth's, third's, are made, as in the two last examples: the bells in front making third's in running in and out, namely, the bells doing the 6,5,6 work.

E

CHAP. IX.—METHODS ON EIGHT BELLS.

DUFFIELD ; *Diagram page* 25.

This useful method, produced in 1886 by Sir Arthur Heywood, Bart., is adaptable to 8, 10, or 12 bells.

The plain course of Major consists of eight similar sixes, the whole being so simple that it would appear possible—after a careful analysis of the diagram—to take a rope and steer oneself through a plain course.

The first row of a six is a back-stroke, so the "go off" falls in with the second row of a six. The whole pulls at the lead and back are "right," and so are the internal places, so the learner is not unduly bothered at the outset.

Double dodging, both at the front and back, is the inflexible rule ; and whether you start from the front or back, you make the far place in the central four-bell work, retrace your steps through three bells to the near place, and then restart on your journey through five bells, and take up the far double dodging ; you then lead, or lie, as the case may be, and make another double dodge, after which you recommence your four-bell work in the other direction, and complete the plain course with the other double dodging work, as shown in the diagram. Being a perfect double method, the work on the way down is an exact reversal of that on the way up. The terms "first third's" and "last third's" are used to express the order in which a ringer makes these places.

Bob.—At a bob (and the same at a single) the bell that is about to leave the four-bell work and go behind, makes sixth's, and recommences the four-bell work ; the others behave exactly as in Stedman. Whatever the number of bells, a call only affects the last three, and it may be here noted that, in extending the method from 8 to 10 and 12 bells, Stedman-work behind is strictly followed both at the plain six-ends, and at those that have calls.

The coloured lines on the diagram have been specially arranged to impress on the eye what Sir Arthur has expressed in so many words. The reader is supposed to be ringing the tenor, which is shown by the thick red line throughout the plain course : your " course-bell " is under the thick blue line, namely the sixth : your " after-bell " (which is that which courses after you) is shown by the thin blue line through the seventh ; whilst your " Double-bell " is shown by the thin red line through the treble.

Your Double-bell.—If the plain course be examined, the thick and thin red lines will be seen to be tracing symmetrical but exactly opposite paths. Thus a ringer, knowing his Double, knows exactly at any moment what that bell should be doing. You pass her in 4-5, both up and down, and can consequently watch her movements. A call does not affect your mutual relationship whilst you are in the four-bell work, but if one be made as you are going down to lead, and a clash occur, you know that your double should be the bob-making bell, and you can help her through.

Your Course-bell.—This is an important aid. You always dodge her first on reaching the back or front, so if, unfortunately, you forget your position, you can, when you come into, say, third's, notice whether she is in the dodging, and if so, join her—if not, turn away again. " In short, never leave the four-bell work until you see your course-bell in the dodging," tersely says Sir Arthur. " The only exception is when she is called to make a bob, and turns back again. There are three positions in which a call will alter your course-bell, but these we must leave the reader to analyse for himself, and, in doing so, notice also how to recognise his new one.

Your " After-bell."—The knowledge of where to strike over her is very useful. You pass her, for instance, in 5-6, when making last sixth's, and cut her in 4-3 when about to make last third's. You also dodge in front and behind with her after dodging with your course-bell. In the four-bell work your course-bell is with you in the first six, and your after-bell during the last.

"To those who possess the power of keeping others straight, the following hints will prove of service : When in the dodging, if anyone tries to join you at the *first* dodge, send him away to the opposite dodging ; if at the second dodge, tell him to make the far (last) place, and come back again ; if it is directly a bob is called—you being behind and making the first of the extra dodges—tell him to go down and make first third's, as he is the bob-making bell." Notice also that the *last* (back-stroke) blow of first third's, or first sixth's, is made at the same time as the last dodge of the bells in front and behind : the last third's and last s xth's being made a whole pull previously. " I may say,"— quoting the author—" that in ' Duffield ' it will be found next to impossible to ring with certainty without watching the course-bell and the double-bell."

For nearly every remark here gleaned we are indebted to Sir Arthur Heywood's Treatise on " The Duffield Method," unfortunately now out of print.

DOUBLE NORWICH COURT ; *Diagram page* 26.

(*The half lead dates from Stedman's time, when fifth's was made with the treble behind, and fourth's with her in front, irregular lead ends resulting. It was then termed College Bob Major, and the present arrangement first appeared in print in the " Clavis," as Norwich Court Bob*).

This is undoubtedly the most musical of all the plain methods, here given, on eight bells, and is at least equal, if not superior, to any other Major method. Considering this, and bearing in mind that it is seldom practised on account of its *supposed* complexity, I here give a fuller description of the duty than would otherwise have been necessary.

Fourth's and third's places are made, by one bell, as the treble passes through 3-4 up ; and sixth's and fifth's, by another, as the treble passes through 5-6 up. Fifth's and sixth's, and third's and fourth's are also made as the treble hunts down. This place-making creates dodges in 3-4 and 5-6 at certain intervals, and invariably causes each bell to make a *double dodge* both before, and after, leading and lying, except when the treble intervenes.

Let us examine the work of the bells before and behind. commencing with the work at the lead. Between each of the different leads of the treble three bells are in front ; of these, one, that turns the treble away, leads, and double dodges after ; and is said to do " *first work in front.*"* The bell that comes in, and double dodges with this first-work bell, leads, and afterwards makes another double dodge ; and is said to do " *full work in front.*" The next (the last of the three) makes a double dodge with this full work bell, leads,

---

* Meaning first work of the whole lead.

and is then turned away by the treble ; and thus does " *last work in front.*" In the same way three bells work behind ; one does " *first work behind,*" another " *full work behind,*" and the last " *last work behind.*" Thus, whenever you come to lead, or go behind, unless you turn the treble away you make a double dodge, lead, or lie, as the case may be, and, unless the treble turns you away, afterwards make another double dodge.

When the bells leave the front, it will be seen that (in the first lead) one bell dodges in 3-4 and 5-6 up ; and (in the fifth lead), when leaving the back, dodges in 5-6 and 3-4 down. This work is, respectively, the duty of bells after finishing *first work*, in front, and behind.

If the other bells, leaving the front, be examined, it will be seen that one bell hunts up into 5-6, where it dodges, makes sixth's and fifth's places, and then hunts up. Another bell hunts up to fourth's, makes fourth's and third's, dodges in 3-4, and then hunts up behind. Concerning these " *place-making bells,*" it should be noted that one dodges *before*, and the other *after*, making the places ; but neither of them dodge in the intermediate places, on their way to, or from, their place-making positions. In other words, the bell that hunts up to make the places in 5-6, although it makes a dodge in 5-6 *before* making these places, does not dodge in 3-4 on its way up to 5-6 ; nor does it dodge in 5-6 *after* making the places. The other bell, which does not dodge *before* making the places in 3-4 up, dodges *after* making them ; but does not dodge in 5-6 on its way behind.

In the same way, of the place-making bells from behind, one runs straight down into 3-4, where it dodges, makes third's and fourth's places, and goes straight to the lead; the other makes fifth's and sixth's places, dodges in 5-6, and goes straight down.

The places made from the front, and back, may be known as the "*far*" and "*near*" places, according to their relationship to the respective starting points. From the front, the places in 5-6 would be the far, and those in 3-4 the near places; from behind, the 3-4 would be the far, and the 5-6 the near, places. The bells that do full work, in front, and behind, proceed to make the far places, and those that do last work in front and behind, make the near places. The far places *begin*, and the near places *end*, with a dodge. These facts can easily be remembered by noticing that bells that have done full work in front, and behind, *leave those positions with a dodge; and begin the place-making with a dodge;* those that have done last work in front, and behind, leave those positions without dodging, and commence the place-making without dodging.

The work of bells from the front and back may be summarised thus :

> After first work, in front, dodge in 3-4, and 5-6, up.
> After full work, in front, make the far places,
> After last work, in front, make the near places.
>
> After first work, behind, dodge in 5-6, and 3-4, down.
> After full work, behind, make the far places.
> After last work, behind, make the near places.

Although the plain-course duty does *not* occur in the above order, the table shows the similarity of the work from the front and back. I advise my readers to question themselves until they can decide, when leaving the front, and back, what duty they have to perform.

The following is another way of considering this duty. The bell that does the first work (before and behind) makes no places, but merely dodges; the bell that does full work goes as far as it can without making the places, that is, it makes the far places; the bell that does last duty *at once* makes the near places.

The order in which the different duties actually occur, as shown below, should now be learnt.

Double Norwich Court.   Duty of each bell in a plain course.

First work in front.   Last work behind.
Full work in front.
First work behind.   Last work in front.
Full work behind.

It will be seen that the *first* work (front and back) is followed by the *last* work in the opposite position; and the last work is always followed by the *full* work. A great variety of observations as to the order of the duties may be made;

	5 3 7 2 8 4 6 1	5 3 7 2 8 4 6 1
	3 5 2 7 4 8 1 6	3 5 2 7 4 8 1 6
	5 3 7 2 4 1 8 6	5 3 7 2 4 1 8 6
	3 5 2 7 1 4 6 8	3 5 2 7 1 4 6 8
	5 3 2 1 7 4 8 6	5 3 2 1 7 4 8 6
	3 5 1 2 4 7 6 8	3 5 1 2 4 7 6 8
	3 1 5 2 7 4 8 6	3 1 5 2 7 4 8 6
BOB	⎰ 1 3 2 5 4 7 6 8	SINGLE ⎰ 1 3 2 5 4 7 6 8
	⎱ 1 2 3 4 5 7 8 6	⎱ 1 2 3 4 5 7 6 8
	2 1 4 3 7 5 6 8	2 1 4 3 7 5 8 6
	2 4 1 3 5 7 8 6	2 4 1 3 5 7 6 8
	4 2 3 1 7 5 6 8	4 2 3 1 7 5 8 6
	2 4 3 7 1 5 8 6	2 4 3 7 1 5 6 8
	4 2 7 3 5 1 6 8	4 2 7 3 5 1 8 6
	2 4 3 7 5 6 1 8	2 4 3 7 5 8 1 6
	4 2 7 3 6 5 8 1	4 2 7 3 8 5 6 1

for instance, if you leave the place-making with a dodge, your work, whether in front or behind, begins with dodging. I shall, however, leave further observations to the ingenuity of my readers, and proceed to consider the calls.

Bob.—At a bob, sixth's place is made ; this causes the bells behind to continue dodging (a five-pull dodge in all) until separated by the treble ; the bells below sixth's place are unaltered ; the others are altered as follows :

A bell, that dodged in 3-4 and 5-6 up, makes sixth's place, and then dodges in 5-6 and 3-4 down.

A bell, that has completed the *first* work behind, makes an additional three-pull dodge there, and becomes the bell that has done *full* work behind.

A bell, that would have done the *full* work behind, makes a five-pull dodge, lies, and becomes the bell that has done the *last* work behind.

Single.—At a single, one bell does full work behind, as at a plain lead ; another makes sixth's place, as at bob ; the bell that has done first work behind makes *seventh's place*, and then begins the last work behind.

DOUBLE OXFORD ; *Diagram page* 27.

(*It will be noticed that the first half lead is, row for row, Double Norwich ; and the Minor, we know, dates from* 1677).

In this, as in Double Norwich Court, third's and fourth's, and fifth's and sixth's places, are made, when the treble is passing through these positions on her way up and down. In Double Oxford, however, second's and seventh's places, respectively, are also made when the treble leads and lies. Bells are thus retained before, and behind, until they have completed all their duty there. The whole duty, which is continuous, is easily learnt therefore in one lesson.

On coming to the lead each bell makes a five-pull dodge, leads, makes second's place, leads, and then makes another five-pull dodge. Work similar to this also occurs behind. On leaving the front, each bell dodges in 3-4, makes fourth's and third's places, and *then* makes a three-pull dodge in 3-4 ; after this it passes into 5-6, where it *begins* with a three-pull dodge, makes sixth's and fifth's places, dodges in 5-6, and then goes up to the work behind. Similar work occurs on the way down from behind.

It will be seen that the three-pull dodges, in 3-4 and 5-6, *follow one another ;* that is, after leaving the front and back, a three-pull dodge takes place *after* the place-making, and then another such dodge immediately precedes the next place-making ; thus the three-pull dodges may be said to occur together.

Bob.—At a bob, fourth's place instead of second's, is made ; the work of the bells in 5-6, and 7-8, is not altered ; that of the others is altered thus :

A bell, that has just left the work in front, makes fourth's place (instead of dodging in 3-4), and goes down to the work in front again.

A bell that would have made second's place, runs out, makes fourth's and third's, dodges three times in 3-4, and goes up to the three-pull dodge, etc., in 5-6.

A bell, that has made the places in 3-4 down, runs straight in (instead of dodging in 3-4) and takes up the remainder of the work in front.

Single.—At a single, one bell makes second's place, as at a plain lead ; another makes fourth's, as at a bob ; and the bell that has made third's and fourth's places on the way down, makes *third's place ;* and then fourth's and third's, etc., on the way up.

CHAP. X.
TREBLE BOB METHODS ON EIGHT BELLS.

ALBION TREBLE BOB MAJOR; *Diagram pages* 32-33.

This fine example of an Imperial Method first appeared in Hubbard, 1845, where it is placed to the credit of Hugh Wright, of Leeds, Yorkshire, the author of that work adding : " It is the most even and regular of any Treble Bob method extant, inasmuch as any peal of Bob Major, with bobs only, and tenors together, may be applied to it." The number of changes would then, of course, be doubled. Hubbard further points out that every alternate pair of the changes in question will be found to constitute the familiar rows of Bob Major.

It will be noticed that whenever a bell comes to lead, or goes behind, " treble work " is expected of it ; and, at the treble's full work, in front, the sixth's and fifth's (and fifth's and sixth's) places are repeated by the same bell, causing a triple dodge in 3-4, with extra dodges behind, before, and after " treble-work." A bell gives a full lead when the treble lies behind, and when that bell is in front second's place is made. Imperial places are made throughout : in 5-6 when the treble is before, and in 3-4 when she is behind.

Bob.—At a bob fourth's (instead of second's) is made by the bell that—having passed the treble in 2-3—would have joined in a *triple* dodge in 3-4. The bells in front run in and out ; that is—the bell left behind by the treble and (after sixth's and fifth's) due to join the triple dodge in 3-4, dodges *once*, and goes in ; whilst the bell that leaves the slow dodges *once* in 3-4, makes fifth's and sixth's, and goes before the treble to the back.

In the following table, regular work is supposed to be understood :

Albion T. B. Major. Duty of a bell in a plain course.

1. On leaving the slow, make third's and fourth's ; and sixth's and fifth's on the way down to the triple dodge in 3-4.

2. Complete this last ; third's & fourth's out, pass the treble in 6-7 ; and sixth's and fifth's, twice over, going down.

3. Complete this repetition ; make third's & fourth's before dodging the treble in 5-6 out, and dodge twice (extra) *after.*

4. Make all four places, both on the way down and on the way up, with two extra dodges *before* the work behind

5. After dodging treble in 5-6 down, make fourth's & third's, and after dodging treble in 3-4 out, make fifth's and sixth's, twice over.

6. Cut treble in 7-6 down, and make fourth's & third's, pass treble in 2-3, and triple dodge in 3-4.

7. Complete this ; & make fifth's & sixth's ; on the way down fourth's and third's ; and he next the treble.

Except at the bob, and otherwise at the treble leads, all (internal) places are made " wrong."

SUPERLATIVE SURPRISE ; *Diagram pages* 34-5.

(*First appeared in the " Clavis," the authors referring to it as " an original composition of* OUR OWN.")

ALTHOUGH undoubtedly the most musical of the Treble Bob methods here given, there is nothing very complicated about it. Should it ever be generally practised, the full merits of its musical properties will doubtless be properly appreciated.

The diagram shows each bell three times in front, and three times behind, in the plain course. If the work of the bells, in front and behind, be examined, it will be seen that each (the treble permitting) makes a double dodge both before and after leading and lying, except when such a dodge is extended to five pulls. If these five-pull dodges are noted as the exceptions, then double dodging becomes the rule.

When the treble leads and lies, second's and seventh's places, respectively, are made ; this, therefore, keeps the same bells before and behind, and their work, therefore, may be described as " *work with treble in front*," and " *work with treble behind.*" This work is similar, whether before, or behind ; the work with the' treble in front running thus :—double dodge, lead, dodge treble, second's place, dodge treble, lead, and double dodge. The work with the treble behind is relatively the same, seventh's being made instead of second's place.

A very critical examination of the place-making, which occurs in 3-4, and 5-6, is necessary. Take that in the first lead of the diagram. It will be seen that, on arriving in 5-6, a dodge is made, followed by sixth's and fifth's, a dodge then takes place with the treble, sixth's and fifth's are again made, and another dodge follows. Up to this point the work in 5-6, before and after dodging with the treble, may be said to be symmetrical ; that is, the dodges and places made, before and after dodging with the treble, are equal.* At this point a sixth's place, and another dodge, is required to complete the place-making in 5-6. An examination of the place-making in 3-4 in the fifth lead shows that that work is also

---

* In Cambridge Surprise, the place-making consists merely of what is here termed, the symmetrical work, and it may therefore be advantageously studied here, as the *additional* place-making will then be more easily understood.

symmetrical as far as the third dodge, when an extra third's place, and another dodge is added. If, however, the place-making in 3-4 in the third lead, and 5-6 in the seventh, be examined, it will be seen that a dodge in 3-4 and a third's place, and a dodge in 5-6 and a sixth's place, have to be made before the remainder of the work is found symmetrical on each side of the treble's dodge. To distinguish these additions, a custom has been introduced of calling them the " *odd* " places ; thus, in the first lead, the " *odd sixth's* " occurs *last*, that is, *after* the symmetrical work ; in the seventh lead, the " *odd sixth's* " occurs *first*, *i.e.*, before the the other place-making. In the same way, in the third lead, we have " *odd third's first*," and in the fifth lead " *odd third's last*." The place-making duty must be thoroughly learnt, so that, knowing whether odd sixth's or third's comes first, or last, each ringer may " count " his blows, and so leave the place-making position correctly. If this be done the last dodge will show him in which direction he has to proceed, whether up or down.

The places to be made, from the front and back, are those farthest away in each case ; and it will be seen that, afterwards, each bell returns to its starting-point. Thus, on leaving the front, the places to be made are those in 5-6, after which you return again to the front. It is evident, therefore, that before you fall into one of the place-making positions, you pass through a dodging place, and, on your return from place-making you again pass through the same dodging place. Now, the question arises, do you dodge at either of these times ? Examine the first lead of the diagram. On the way to make the places in 5-6, the second bell dodges in 3-4 up ; but, on the way down again, the dodge in 3-4 is omitted. In the third lead, the dodge in 5-6, on the way down to make the places in 3-4, is omitted ; but, in hunting up, this dodge is made. A simple rule, however,' is at hand. If the " odd place " be made *first* you *omit the dodge on the way* to it ; if. however, the odd place be made *last*, you dodge on the way to the place-making position, but come straight away from it.

Having now considered (1) the work with the treble in front, and behind, and also (2) the place-making positions, there only remains to examine (3) the intermediate work between these latter positions. This work is that between the place-making in 5-6 in the first, and that in 3-4 in the third lead ; and between the place-making in the fifth and seventh leads.

In leaving the place-making in the first lead, odd sixth's being made last, the dodge in 3-4 is omitted. Now the work from the point at which the bell shown in the diagram comes to lead, until it leaves the back to make the " odd-third's-first-places " in the third lead, is the intermediate work. It runs thus :—double dodge before leading, and five-pull dodge after ; run straight out ; five-pull dodge before lying, and double-dodge after. The intermediate work in the fifth and sixth leads is simply the reverse, as the first five-pull dodge is made after lying, and you run straight down to the five-pull dodge before leading.

It will be seen that the five-pull dodges follow one another, being separated only by a " run through." In other words, if you leave the work in front with a five-pull dodge, you run straight up and begin the work behind with a five-pull dodge, and *vice versa*.

The whole duty in a plain course is summarised below. Each ringer must make himself perfectly familiar with the details of all the work included in, and connected with, these shortened headings.

Superlative Surprise. Duty of each bell in a plain course.

Work with treble in front.

Odd sixth's last ....Long dodge last (before).

Long dodge first (behind) ....Odd third's first.

Work with treble behind.

Odd third's last ....Long dodge last (behind).

Long dodge first (before) ..Odd sixth's first.

Bob.—At a bob, fourth's place, instead of second's, is made ; the bells above fourth's are not altered ; the others are altered as follows :

A bell, that made " odd third's first," makes *fourth's place,* and takes up the work of the bell making " odd third's last."

A bell, that would have made second's place, runs straight up into 5-6, where it dodges, and hunts up to work with the treble behind.

A bell, that has been with the treble behind, and has dodged in 5-6 down (and was about to make " odd third's last ") runs straight through 3-4 and takes up the remainder of the work with the treble in front.

Cambridge Surprise ; *Diagram pages* 36-7.

(*First found in this correct (Major) form in the " Clavis "*).

Although this method has only been practised by advanced companies, it will not prove to be particularly intricate, as the place-making is simple and regular. The work requiring most study is that into which each bell falls before and after making the different sets of places.

When the treble leads, and lies, second's and seventh's places, respectively, are made. This keeps the same bells before, and behind, and causes them to do " *full work in front* " and " *full work behind.*" The bell that comes down to the full work in front, dodges before and after leading ; and its work so far, being similar to the treble's at the lead, may be called " *treble work.*" After doing this " treble work " such a bell makes second's place, leads, dodges with the treble, makes second's place (over the treble), and repeats the work in reverse order. This work may, therefore, be learnt thus :

Full work in front.

Treble work,	second's,	lead.
Dodge treble,	second's place,	dodge treble.
Lead,	second's,	treble work.

The corresponding full work behind is even more simple, as it consists of a double dodge before lying, after which the treble comes up and has to be dodged with, seventh's place is then made, and the work repeated in reverse order. This work may, therefore, be learnt thus :

Full work behind.

Double dodge, lie, and dodge with the treble.

Seventh's place.

Dodge with the treble, lie, and double dodge.

An examination of the place-making positions in 5-6 and 3-4 up, and in 3-4 and 5-6 down, shows that the work in each of these positions is similar ; that is, you begin with a dodge, make two places, dodge with the treble, then make the same two places and finish with a dodge, after which you continue coursing in your previous path. The bell in the diagram first makes the place in 5-6 up, and then (in the next lead) those in 3-4 up ; after this it does the full work behind, and then makes the places in 3-4 and in 5-6 down.

F

The intermediate work connecting these sets of places requires a little attention. This duty consists in doing "treble work" behind. or before, hunting straight across, and then doing treble work before, or behind. The duty as it occurs in the second and third leads may be set out and learnt thus :

Intermediate work connecting the place-making.

Places in 5-6 up.	Treble work behind.	Places in 3-4 up.
	Run straight across	
	Treble work in front.	

This work connecting the places must be so learnt as to require no further setting out in the plain course duty. Each ringer must therefore remember that when the duty runs thus :

Places in 5-6 up, etc. Places in 3-4 up.

he has this connecting work to insert to complete the whole.

Each bell, after making the sets of places, in 5-6 and 3-4 up, does the full work behind ; after which the places in 3-4 down are made, and the intermediate work (in reverse order) connects them to those that follow in 5-6 down.

It now only remains to learn the other class of inter-mediate work which (1) falls between the full work in front and the place-making in 5-6 up ; and (2) that which falls between the place-making in 5-6 down and the full work in front. The simplest way is to consider it as based on dodging in each place, with "treble work" in front and behind ; and then to observe the omissions and additions that have to be made. These latter, after the work in front, run thus : Omit the dodge in 5-6, but make a double dodge behind. Omit the dodge in 3-4, and before leading. This may be tabulated and learnt thus :

(1) *Intermediate duty after full work in front.*

Omit 5-6. Double dodge behind.
Omit 3-4, and before

Similarly the reverse duty between the place-making and the full work in front may be learnt thus :

(2) *Intermediate duty after place-making in* 5-6 *down.*

Omit after, and 3-4.
Double dodge after. Omit 5-6.

When the details of all the work, and their relative positions, have been carefully studied, the duty of the plain course may be stated as follows ·

Cambridge Surprise. Duty of each bell in a plain course.

Leave full work in front.
Intermediate duty.
Places in 5-6 up, etc. Places in 3-4 up.
Full work behind
Places in 3-4 down, etc. Places in 5-6 down.
Intermediate duty.
Full work in front.

Bob.—At a bob, fourth's place, instead of second's, is made ; the bells above fourth's place are not altered. The others are altered as follows :

A bell, that has made the places in 3-4 up, makes *fourth's*, and then makes the places in 3-4 down, and thus omits the full work behind.

A bell, that would have made second's place, runs straight up into 5-6, dodges there, and goes up to the full work behind.

A bell, that has just completed the full work behind, and is on its way to the place-making in 3-4 down, omits the dodge in 3-4, runs straight in, and takes up the remainder of the full work in front.

London Surprise ; *Diagram pages* 38-9.

(*From the " Clavis."*)

This is, without doubt, an extremely complicated method, a peal in which requires great practice. The conventional way to master the method is to learn the work of a bell in each lead of the plain course. Although not practically acquainted with the method, it would seem to be a better plan to learn the work after (1) meeting the treble on one's way up, and (2) after crossing her path on the way down, as this divides the duty into a series of short lessons.

In tabulating these lessons the work with the treble in front is classed as *work in front*. The term *treble work* has been previously described. The snaps, which are all double, except those at the lead, have their respective strokes set out in each case. Amongst the positions which should be traced on the diagram are four wrong third's places and four wrong pulls behind when the treble is before—all other whole pulls behind being right ; and also four wrong sixth's, and eight wrong leads, when she is behind. There are also three right fifth's when she is behind (or nearly so), one being central, with one before and another after dodging with her in 5-6. Fourth's, and third's, right, are made before and after dodging with the treble in 3-4, both up and down ; and four fourth's wrong, are also made, *i.e.*, two when she is working through 5-6 up, and two when she is working through 5-6 down. In the third lead of the diagram the Stedman whole pulls fall in last-whole-turn style, and in the fifth lead in first-whole-turn style. In learning the duty it should be noted that the central lead of the diagram is symmetrical, and that the first half of the course repeats itself in a reverse order very plainly visible.

The figures in the table in brackets denote the lead then entered upon.

Concise duty, after leaving the full work in front :

	—(**1**) Fourth's ; lead ; fifth's.
Dodge treble 5-6 up	—8, 7, 8 ; third's : (**2**) 6, 5, 6.
Cut treble 5-4 down	—Fourth's ; lead ; sixth's.
Pass treble 6-7 up	—Treble work behind & 7, 8, 8 : (**3**) third's.
Cut treble 3-2 down	—Whole turn ; sixth's.
Dodge treble 7-8 up	—Treble work , 5, 6, 5 ; lie : (**4**) fourth's.
Dodge treble 3-4 down	—Third's ; lead ; fifth's ; lead , third's.
Dodge treble 3-4 up	—Fourth's ; lie : (**5**) 5, 6, 5 ; treble work.
Dodge treble 7-8 down	—Sixth's ; whole turn.
Pass treble 2-3 up	—Third's ; (**6**) 8, 8, 7 & treble work.
Cut treble 7-6 down	—Sixth's ; lead ; fourth's.
Pass treble 4-5 up	—6, 5, 6 , third's ; (**7**) 8. 7, 8.
Dodge treble 5-6 down	—Fifth's ; lead ; fourth's, and full work in front.

Bob.—At a bob, fourth's instead of second's is made ; the bells above being unaltered. The others are altered thus :

A bell, that completed the full work in front during the previous lead (and has just dodged the treble in 5-6 up), after striking 8, 7, 8, hunts down and makes fourth's ; hunts up behind, strikes 8, 7, 8, dodges the treble in 5-6 down, and then goes down to the intermediate and full work in front. The work of this bell is therefore thrown back two leads.

A bell, doing full work in front, instead of making second's place makes third's place, strikes 6, 5, 6, and has its work advanced a lead.

A bell, that passed the treble in 4-5 up, after striking 6, 5, 6, and making third's place, takes up the remainder of the full work in front, and thus has its work advanced a lead.

CHAP. XI.—EXTENTS AND PEALS.
FIVE AND SIX BELLS.

In order to render this work more complete, examples are annexed, in the first place, of Doubles and Minor; leaving Triples and Major to follow. These peals are given by the lead-ends, the mark " — " being used to signify a bob, and the letter S a single.

Plain Methods on Five Bells.

PLAIN BOB.	ST. SIMON'S.	NEW DOUBLES.	STEDMAN'S S.C.
120	120	120	120
2 3 4 5	2 3 4 5	2 3 4 5	2 3 4 5
3 5 2 4	4 2 5 3	3 5 2 4	5 2 3 4
5 4 3 2	5 4 3 2	5 4 3 2	−3 5 4 2
4 2 5 3	3 5 2 4	4 2 5 3	2 3 5 4
−4 2 3 5	−4 2 3 5	−4 2 3 5	4 2 3 5

Each to be twice repeated.

GRANDSIRE.
120
2 3 4 5

2 5 3 4
−3 4 2 5
3 5 4 2
−4 2 3 5
4 5 2 3
S 3 2 4 5
Repeated.

Stedman's and Carter's Doubles.—To complete the extent of these, two singles have to be called when the same two bells are behind. In the diagrams (pages 40 and 41), the two singles for a peal with the fourth and fifth, and the treble and second respectively, behind, are shown; other bells can, however, be chosen to call by.

Plain Methods on Six Bells.

PLAIN BOB.	ST. CLEMENT'S. DOUBLE OXFORD.	DOUBLE COURT.	COLLEGE SINGLE REVERSE.
2 3 4 5 6	2 3 4 5 6	2 3 4 5 6	2 3 4 5 6
-2 3 5 6 4	4 2 6 3 5	5 6 3 4 2	-6 4 2 3 5
3 6 2 4 5	6 4 5 2 3	4 2 6 3 5	5 2 3 6 4
6 4 3 5 2	5 6 3 4 2	3 5 2 6 4	4 3 6 5 2
4 5 6 2 3	-2 3 5 6 4	-6 4 2 3 5	-2 6 4 3 5
-4 5 2 3 6	-4 5 2 3 6	3 5 4 2 6	5 4 3 2 6
-4 5 3 6 2	2 4 6 5 3	-2 6 4 3 5	-6 3 5 4 2
5 6 4 2 3	6 2 3 4 5	3 5 6 4 2	2 5 4 6 3
6 2 5 3 4	3 6 5 2 4	4 2 5 6 3	3 4 6 2 5
2 3 6 4 5	-4 5 3 6 2	-6 3 5 4 2	5 6 2 3 4
3 4 2 5 6	3 4 2 5 6	4 2 3 5 6	4 2 3 5 6

CANTERBURY PLEASURE.	DOUBLE BOB.	GRANDSIRE.
2 3 4 5 6	2 3 4 5 6	2 3 4 5 6
3 5 2 6 4	5 6 3 4 2	-6 5 2 4 3
5 6 3 4 2	4 2 6 3 5	6 4 5 3 2
-6 4 2 3 5	-2 3 5 6 4	-2 3 6 5 4*
4 3 6 5 2	6 4 3 5 2	-4 5 2 6 3
3 5 4 2 6	-4 5 2 3 6	-3 6 4 2 5
5 2 3 6 4	3 6 5 2 4	-5 2 3 4 6
-2 6 4 3 5	2 4 6 5 3	5 4 2 6 3
-6 3 5 4 2	-4 5 3 6 2	-3 6 5 2 4
3 4 6 2 5	'6 2 5 3 4	3 2 6 4 5
4 2 3 5 6	3 4 2 5 6	3 4 2 5 6

If each of the foregoing parts be twice repeated the bells will come round at the half-peal end. If a single is called at the first half-peal end, and the whole repeated, the 720 changes will be produced.

In Plain Bob, St. Clement's, Double Oxford, and Double Bob, if the singles are called at the half-peal ends the tenors will not be reversed. If the single in Double Court is called at the first lead-end, in College Single at the ninth, and in

Canterbury pleasure at the second lead-end, in one of tho parts of the first half-peal, the tenors will not be reversed ; the second single must of course be called in the corresponding part in the second half of the peal. In the Grandsire example a single may be substituted for a bob at the third lead-end (*see* *) in one part of each half-peal, without disturbing the tenors.

The foregoing peals are called by the observation of the fifth and sixth bells. In the methods in which the bells behind are undisturbed by the bobs, the tenor is called when behind without the fifth ; the singles have then to be called when these two bells are behind. In methods in which the two bells in front are not altered, the bobs have to be called when the tenor is in second's or third's place at the lead-end without the fifth in the other of these positions ; the singles have then to be called at a lead-end when the tenors are in front.

Treble Bob Methods on Six Bells.

OXFORD. KENT. ·	OLD OXFORD. COL. BOB IV. SOUTHWARK. LONDON S.	WESTMINSTER. YORK S. CARLISLE S. CHESTER S.	COLLEGE EXERCISE.
2 3 4 5 6	2 3 4 5 6	2 3 4 5 6	2 3 4 5 6
4 2 6 3 5	4 2 6 3 5	-2 3 5 6 4	6 4 5 2 3
-6 4 2 3 5	6 4 5 2 3	3 6 2 4 5	-2 3 5 6 4
-2 6 4 3 5	5 6 3 4 2	6 4 3 5 2	4 5 6 2 3
4 2 5 6 3	-2 3 5 6 4	4 5 6 2 3	3 6 2 4 5
5 4 3 2 6	-4 5 2 3 6	-4 5 2 3 6	-4 5 2 3 6
3 5 6 4 2	2 4 6 5 3	-4 5 3 6 2	6 2 3 4 5
-6 3 5 4 2	6 2 3 4 5	5 6 4 2 3	-4 5 3 6 2
5 6 2 3 4	3 6 5 2 4	6 2 5 3 4	2 3 6 4 5
2 5 4 6 3	-4 5 3 6 2	2 3 6 4 5	5 6 4 2 3
4 2 3 5 6	3 4 2 5 6	3 4 2 5 6	3 4 2 5 6

In the methods in which the bells going into and coming out of the slow (or the work in front) are undisturbed by the bobs, the peals are called by the observation of the tenor in and out without the fifth. In the methods in which the bells behind are the ones not altered by the bobs, the tenor is called when behind without the fifth.

TULIP. CAMBRIDGE S BEVERLEY S.	KENTISH DELIGHT.	CANTERBURY SURPRISE
2 3 4 5 6	2 3 4 5 6	2 3 4 5 6
5 6 3 4 2	3 5 2 6 4	6 4 5 2 3
4 2 6 3 5	5 6 3 4 2	-2 3 5 6 4
-2 3 5 6 4	-6 4 2 3 5	4 5 6 2 3
6 4 3 5 2	4 3 6 5 2	3 6 2 4 5
-4 5 2 3 6	3 5 4 2 6	-4 5 2 3 6
3 6 5 2 4	5 2 3 6 4	6 2 3 4 5
2 4 6 5 3	-2 6 4 3 5	-4 5 3 6 2
-4 5 3 6 2	-6 3 5 4 2	2 3 6 4 5
6 2 5 3 4	3 4 6 2 5	5 6 4 2 3
3 4 2 5 6	4 2 3 5 6	3 4 2 5 6

Each of the preceding parts has to be twice repeated.

Peals of Triples and Major.—In Plain Bob, etc., M.W.H. or W.M.H., as the case may be, refer to the three hindermost positions of the tenor; and in Double Oxford and Superlatives, B, in these headings, denotes a call with the tenors "Before." In Grandsire, the numbers following a course-end denote the number of leads since the previous call. In Stedman's Triples an explanation of the calling is given below the figures. In Duffield, I.B.O. will be found on the diagram, as In, Before, Out; whilst the figures in the heading of Double Norwich refer to the number of the lead-ends of any particular course.

GRANDSIRE TRIPLES.
5040.

Calling of First Half.		Calling of Second Half.	
234567		235476	
752634	1	642735	1
347265	2	740523	5
243576	5	547362	5
542637	5	345276	5
765342	1	763524	2
367254	5	567432	5
543726	2	245367	1
745632	5	342756	5
647253	5	743625	5
246375	5	257364	2

Repeat first half four times, with S. for B. at the half-peal end; then call the second half, and repeat it four times, with S. for B. at the end.

(Holt's Singles—*see page* 10.)

JOHN HOLT.

BOB MAJOR
5040

23456	W	M	H
43652	-	-	
64235		-	
20543	-	-	-
52364		-	
35420		-	
45623	-	-	
64352		-	
36245		-	
23564		-	
52436		-	
42635	-	-	
64523		-	
56342		-	
35264		-	-
42356	-	-	-

Three times repeated.

B. ANNABLE.

PLAIN BOB TRIPLES.
5040

23456	M	W	H
64235	-	-	-
26435			
42635			
63425	-		
46325			
34625			

Nine times repeated, with a Single for a Bob at the fifth and tenth part ends.

H. HUBBARD.

A bob is shown by (—); consecutive bobs by numbers, as in Oxford; and a single instead of a bob, is shown by an S. The calling marks might with greater correctness be given in front of the course-end, as the figures are the *results* of the calls.

STEDMAN'S TRIPLES.

5040.

Transposition of Thurstans' " Master-piece "—(Twenty Parts), by Sir Arthur Heywood, Bart.

2 3 1 4 5 6	(2 3 1 4 5 6) S L S14
3 4 6 1 2 5 S at 2	4 3 5 2 1 6 L*omitted
4 1 3 2 6 5 S H Q	3 2 4 1 5 6 Standard
1 4 3 2 5 6 H	2 1 3 5 4 6 ,,
3 5 1 2 4 6 Extra (L)	1 5 2 4 3 6 ,,
5 2 3 4 1 6 Standard	5 4 1 3 2 6 ,,
2 4 5 1 3 6 ,,	3 4 2 5 1 6 L*omitted
4 1 2 3 5 6 ,,	4 5 3 1 2 6 Standard
1 3 4 5 2 6 ,,	5 1 4 2 3 6 ,,
4 2 1 5 3 6 Extra (L)	1 2 5 3 4 6 ,,
2 5 4 3 1 6 Standard	2 3 1 4 5 6 ,,
5 3 2 1 4 6 ,,	
3 1 5 4 2 6 ,,	

THOMAS THURSTANS.

The standard calling of each three-course-division is given below: the L* is the one to omit on the two occasions set out, and the (L) is that twice intro-duced as the extra.

(1) S   L* ⎫
(2) S   H   ⎬ Q ⎰ All bobs are
(3)   H   (L) ⎭   ⎱ in pairs :

S denotes In slow & first whole turn.
H   ..   First & Second half turns.
L   ,,   Last whole turn & out.
Q   ,,   In & out, quick.

DUFFIELD MAJOR.

5000

	I	B	O.
1 2 3 4 5			
4 3 2 1 5	–	–	.
2 4 3 1 5		–	
5 2 4 1 3		s	–
4 5 2 1 3		–	
3 2 5 1 4		–	
5 3 2 1 4		–	
2 5 3 1 4		–	
4 3 5 1 2		–	–
5 4 3 1 2		–	
3 5 4 1 2		–	
2 4 5 1 3		–	–

These eleven courses, eight times repeated, substituting Bobs for the Single except in the sixth part, produce :

4 5 1 2 3			
2 1 5 4 3	–		–
5 2 1 4 3			–
3 1 2 4 5		–	–
2 3 1 4 5			–
5 1 3 4 2		–	–
1 2 5 3 6 4 H			

Round at two changes.

A.P.H., Sept., 1886.

D. NORWICH C.B. 5376

2 3 4 5 6	1	4	6
3 5 6 2 4	s	—	—
5 6 3 2 4	—	—	—
6 3 5 2 4	—	—	—
3 2 5 6 4	—	—	—

Eleven times repeated, with S. for B. at 6 in the third course of the sixth and twelfth parts.

JOHN CARTER.

OXFORD. 5120.

2 3 4 5 6	M	W	H
5 6 3 4 2	1	2	2
5 3 4 6 2	2	1	2
5 4 6 3 2	2	1	2

Four times repeated.

J. REEVES.

DOUBLE OXFORD. 5120.

2 3 4 5 6	M	B	H
4 3 5 2 6	—	—	—
5 3 2 4 6	—	—	—
5 3 4 6 2	—	—	—
4 5 3 6 2	—	—	—
3 4 5 6 2	—	—	—

Nine times repeated, with S. for B. at the end of the fifth and tenth parts.

REV. J. H. PILKINGTON.

KENT. 5280.

2 3 4 5 6	M	W	H
3 6 4 5 2	1	—	2
6 3 2 5 4	2	—	2
5 2 3 6 4	—	2	2
5 3 6 2 4	—	1	2
2 5 3 4 6	2	—	2

Twice repeated.

HENRY JOHNSON.

SUPERLATIVE SURPRISE. 5120.

2 3 4 5 6	B	M	H
2 3 5 6 4	—	—	—
5 2 3 6 4	—	—	—
3 5 2 6 4	—	—	—
4 2 5 6 3	—	—	—
5 4 2 6 3	—	—	—

Four times repeated.

H. JOHNSON.

ALBION. 5376.

2 3 4 5 6	W	M	H
6 4 2 3 5	—	—	—
2 6 4 3 5	—	—	—
4 2 6 3 5	—	—	—
5 6 2 3 4	—	—	—
2 3 5 6 4	—	—	—
5 2 3 6 4	—	—	—
3 5 2 6 4	—	—	—
4 2 3 5 6	—	—	—

Twice repeated.

HUGH WRIGHT.

CAMBRIDGE SURPRISE. 5600.

2 3 4 5 6	M	W	H
4 3 6 5 2	—	—	—
5 6 2 3 4	2	—	—
2 3 5 6 4	—	—	—
5 2 3 6 4	—	—	—
3 5 2 6 4	—	—	—

Four times repeated.

C. MIDDLETON.

LONDON SURPRISE. 5600.

2 3 4 5 6	M	W	H
6 5 4 3 2	—	—	—
4 6 5 3 2	—	—	—
2 3 5 6 4	—	—	—
5 2 3 6 4	—	—	—
3 5 2 6 4	—	—	—

Four times repeated.

J. REEVES

'tning Source UK Ltd.
` Keynes UK
920751010323
'K00006B/284